Praise for *When the Spirit Is Your Inheritance*

This is one of the best, most illuminating and engaging of the many books I have read on Latino Pentecostalism. It is deeply appreciative and committed to Pentecostal faith and tradition, but not uncritical of it. It includes valuable comments and examples of that typical Pentecostal genre known as "testimonios." But—and this is what I find most engaging—it itself is a brilliant, lifelong, and heartfelt testimonio!

—Justo L. González, author of *Mañana: Christian Theology from a Hispanic Perspective* and *The Story of Christianity*

Calvillo's *When the Spirit Is Your Inheritance* is a brilliant, insider's perspective of Latino Pentecostalism at the borderlands. Sharing his own family's powerful narratives and employing his sociological imagination, he portrays and analyzes the ways that borders have shaped his Pentecostal spirituality while also offering spaces to create and establish new callings and ministries. This autoethnography provides keen insights on how the Spirit moves at the intersection of race, ethnicity, and empire.

—Russell Jeung, professor of Asian American studies, San Francisco State University

A compelling narrative at the intersection of borderlands and Pentecostalism that demonstrates how these interact to refashion each other, providing insights, illumination, and inspiration for pneumatology, finding the divine in the human, and blazing new ways to traverse the borderlands. A reading for scholars, immigrants, preachers, everyday pilgrims, and prophets.

—Elizabeth Conde-Frazier, practical theologian, Association for Hispanic Theological Education

When the Spirit Is Your Inheritance opens a new de-centering vista in the study of Pentecostalism and borderlands. Jonathan Calvillo has expanded what is usually a scholar's footnote or introductory sentence into a full-fledged model of self-reflexivity, turning the ethnographic gaze inward, as well as outward toward the community that shaped and is being studied by the scholar. With the descriptive power of a James Baldwin and the introspection of a Richard Rodríguez, Calvillo offers a deeper understanding of the personal and social dimensions of spirit-empowerment among the ostensibly peripheral and disempowered, beyond glossolalia or other usual markers of Pentecostal identity and practice.

—Daniel Ramírez, author of *Migrating Faith:*
Pentecostalism in the United States and Mexico
in the Twentieth Century

For the first time, in this important new book by noted Latinx religion scholar Jonathan Calvillo, I find my own lived experience of borderlands spirituality and culture reflected in the genre of memoir. With the analytic eye of a leading sociologist of religion, combined with the engaging prose of an artist, Calvillo movingly captures how the "Spirit in the borderlands" has been a source of strength and resilience for so many of our Latinx families in the face of cultural dislocation and ongoing change.

—Robert Chao Romero, associate professor,
Department of Chicana/o and Central American
Studies, University of California, Los Angeles

In *When the Spirit Is Your Inheritance*, Jonathan Calvillo delivers excellent and nuanced insights about contextualized Pentecostalism through the lens of both literal and conceptual borderlands, weaving together big stories and little stories that also provide insights for other faith-based communities. Drawing on his research and the experiences of transnational *testimonios* across many generations, Calvillo presents a sweeping nonbinary analysis well-grounded in particular accounts as well historical and sociological realities. It helps us examine the workings of power at micro and macro levels through the experiences of borderlands Pentecostals.

—Edwin David Aponte, dean of the Theological School,
and professor of religion and culture,
Drew University

When the Spirit Is Your Inheritance

When the Spirit Is
YOUR INHERITANCE

Reflections
on
Borderlands Pentecostalism

Jonathan Calvillo

FORTRESS PRESS
MINNEAPOLIS

WHEN THE SPIRIT IS YOUR INHERITANCE
Reflections on Borderlands Pentecostalism

29 28 27 26 25 24   1 2 3 4 5 6 7 8 9

Library of Congress Control Number: 2024937753 (print)

Cover image: compilation of stock illustrations from Getty Images
Cover design: Kristin Miller

Print ISBN: 979-8-8898-3037-5
eBook ISBN: 979-8-8898-3038-2

To my parents, Alvaro and Lydia Calvillo, gracias
por la fundación que han vivido.
To my familia—Puanani, Kalea, Mahalia, and
Jonathan—thank you for your creativity.
To those who have crossed,
Para aquellos que han cruzado,
to those who are crossing,
para aquellos que están cruzando,
to those on the brink of crossing,
para aquellos que están por cruzar,
to those who do not ultimately cross,
para aquellos que al final no cruzan,
and to those ever crossing,
y para aquellos que siempre están cruzando,
may the breath you need be ever with you
que el suspiro que necesiten este siempre con ustedes.

Contents

Contents

Acknowledgments

I am grateful for the support I have received from my colleagues at Emory University and Candler School of Theology. In particular, I am grateful to Joanne Solis-Walker, Tony Alonso, Ish Ruiz, María Carrión, Helen Jin Kim, Roger Nam, Nicole Renée Phillips, Jan Love, Ted Smith, Jacob L. Wright, James Abbington, Bo Adams, Jennifer R. Ayres, Sarah Bogue, Ryan Bonfiglio, Elizabeth M. Bounds, Anthony A. Briggman, Letitia M. Campbell, Elizabeth Corrie, David B. Daniel, Kyrah Malika Daniels, L. Wesley de Souza, Musa W. Dube, Thomas W. Elliott Jr., Gregory C. Ellison II, Robert M. Franklin Jr., Teresa L. Fry Brown, Geoffrey Goodman, Larry M. Goodpaster, Alison Collis Greene, Jehu J. Hanciles, Danielle Tumminio Hansen, Susan E. Hylen, Arun W. Jones, Joel Kemp, Kyle Lambelet, Kwok Pui Lan, Emmanuel Y. Lartey, Joel M. LeMon, Lahronda Little, Steffen Lösel, Ellen Ott Marshall, Joy Ann McDougall, Ian McFarland, Keith Menhinick, Brett Opalinski, Susan Reynolds, R. Kendall Soulen, Dianne Stewart, Jonathan Strom, Gabrielle Thomas, Khalia J. Williams, Walter T. Wilson, and Deanna Ferree Womack.

I am also thankful for additional friends and colleagues who have remained in conversation through the process of writing this book: Daniel Ramírez, Erica Ramirez, Lloyd Barba, Leah Payne, Sammy Alfaro, Ekaputra Tupamahu, Andrea Johnson, Roy Fisher, Marla Frederick, Filipe Maia, Mark Villegas, Edwin Johnson, Daniel White Hodge, Jon Gill, Yara Gonzalez, Cristian De La Rosa, Patrick Reyes, Xavier Pickett, Robert Chao Romero, Jorge Juan Rodriguez, Daniel Camacho, Tony Lin, and Nicollete Manglos-Weber.

Of particular help in regard to my sociological outlook have been conversations with Aida Ramos, Gerardo Martí, Mark Mulder,

ACKNOWLEDGMENTS

Melissa Guzman Garcia, Ryon Cobb, Yader Lanuza, and Brad Christerson.

To the members of the extended Calvillo family and Sanchez-Fraijo family, you were a constant inspiration for this book.

David and Ernesto, thank you for your ongoing support.

Last but not least, thank you to my editor, Bethany Dickerson, for her attention to detail, insightful suggestions, and ongoing dialogue.

Introduction

The Spirit en La Frontera

My mother, Lydia, was surprised by the peculiar letters scrawled within a Bible belonging to her mother-in-law, my grandmother, Adelina "Ama" Calvillo. My mother inquired, "Hermana, usted sabe quién escribió esto?" ["Sister, do you know who wrote this?"] The letters in question, written on one of the first pages of my grandmother's Bible, read *F. T. T.*

"Si, yo lo escribí" ["Yes, I wrote it"], my grandmother replied.

"Y usted sabe que quiere decir?" ["And do you know what it means?"] my mother pressed further.

"Pues Fullerton!" ["Well, Fullerton!"] my grandmother asserted.

My mother explained that *FTT* stood for the local gang.[1] My grandmother noticed these letters written around the neighborhood and associated them with the town she and her family had migrated to in around 1976. Her markings were intended to let people know where the Bible belonged, marking her faith as grounded and alive in the social borderlands where the Spirit had allowed her to settle.

My grandmother Adelina had laid down roots in Fullerton, California, specifically in the old Mexican barrio on Truslow Street. Her faith was grounded in the day-to-day spaces that she inhabited—*en lo cotidiano*.[2] She had read the writing on the wall and repurposed it within her Bible. She had brought together sacred Scripture and street scripts.[3] Her faith had an address.[4] My grandmother's faith had endured across migration routes, from the Mexican state of Chihuahua to stints in Texas, New Mexico, and California, with multiple back-and-forth circulations, ultimately laying roots in California. By marking her Bible with the turf of her new town, she signaled that she and her faith belonged there.

By settling in California, my grandmother and the rest of the Calvillo family were not relinquishing their spiritual ties to their borderland homelands; the Spirit *en la frontera* moved within them to new *fronteras*—new borderlands. Indeed, the Spirit to them was of the borderlands. My grandmother's spiritual practices and cosmologies, the brand of Pentecostal Christianity that she brought from the Texas-Chihuahua borderlands, found a home in Southern California. And as with the markings in her Bible, through migration and adaptation, a variety of additional expressions, sacred and profane, came to mark her faith and that of her household. She had moved from one borderland to another borderland, demarcated as the proverbial "other side of the tracks." And through these borderlands, the Spirit moved.

CIRCULATIONS

My grandmother Ama was born into a spiritual borderlands, a space where cosmovisions[5] converged, sometimes giving rise to hybridized practices[6] and sometimes energizing people to seek new pathways altogether. Her parents, Esequiel Macias and Dolores Gomez, were married in 1921 at Templo de San Antonio de Padua, a Franciscan mission founded in 1696 in what would become Casas Grandes, Chihuahua. A mile from the mission rests Paquime, once the center of trade, culture, and spiritual devotion for the native peoples of the region from the twelfth to the fifteenth centuries.[7] Arguably, the most important archaeological site of Northern Mexico, Paquime was itself a place of confluence. There, archaeologists unearthed pottery from the native peoples of the US Southwest alongside artifacts depicting Mesoamerican deities. At Paquime, the cultures of southern Mesoamerica converged with those of the Southwest pueblos. This site[8] where peoples, cultures, and spiritual knowledge circulated was near where Ama was born and spent her first years.

Ama's father died an early death, and her mother soon remarried, introducing another spiritual element into their lives. Her new stepfather was a man of mystery, trained in forms of magic and healing. She recalled a lone photo of him from her childhood in which he stood holding a hand over a black book. Ama remembered that people would seek him out to be treated for their ailments, repaying him with money and sometimes with other valuable items. After a few years, he, too, would pass away; her mother, Dolores, remarried again.

Dolores's third marriage set off a series of moves for Ama, with the next stage of her life involving ongoing movement, eventually to the US-Mexico border. Living in a remote town in the Sierra of Chihuahua, Ama helped Dolores run a rustic diner that served truckers and lumber workers connected to the local lumber industry. While working there, she met my grandfather Fermin "Apa" Calvillo, who drove lumber to the cities below. After the two married, Ama sometimes traveled with Apa on his deliveries, helping in various ways, such as driving home a car that they purchased on a trip. The two settled in Casas Grandes, where my father was born, and then moved to the border city of Ciudad Juárez. She had eleven children, and she and Apa adopted two of their nephews who had been orphaned.

While they were living in Ciudad Juárez, Ama's spiritual borderlands journey took an important turn. Her sister, Hermila, living in Casas Grandes, had been introduced to Pentecostalism and began to share with Ama about her new encounters with God. Hermila would often write letters to Ama, telling her about the love of God that she experienced and encouraging her to give it a try. Eventually, Hermila came to visit Ama in person to share with her about her new faith experience. Soon after, Ama began to visit a local Pentecostal church and had a conversion experience. She committed her life to following Jesus Christ and became Pentecostal. She would continue to cross borders, but she had found her spiritual home. As the first Pentecostal in her household, she cultivated this form of Christianity, centered on the Holy Spirit, among her family members,[9] seeking the guidance of the Spirit wherever she went.

FORGED IN THE BORDERLANDS

My family's spiritual journeys were made all the more dynamic by their ties to Borderlands Pentecostalism, a Pentecostalism forged in the superhighway of spiritual exchange that is the US-Mexico border region. Religion scholar Rudy Busto[10] describes the US-Mexico border region as a type of burned-over district, a "frontera quemada," which at the turn of the twentieth century was home to a bustling religious ecology. The demarcation of the US-Mexico border and the territories carved out in US conquest significantly shaped the religious futures of peoples in the borderlands. Targeting its primarily Catholic population, concerted missionary efforts from Protestants facilitated through US territorial acquisitions gave way to localized and indigenized Protestant, evangelical, and Pentecostal traditions. While missionary efforts were often tainted by racialized hierarchical ideologies that marginalized Natives,[11] Hispanos, and Mexican Nationals, localized religious communities ultimately emerged from these efforts.

By the time my parents' families joined Pentecostal churches, these were communities led by locals, rather than outsiders, reflecting significant aspects of local borderlands culture. Historical patterns of migrant labor recruitment and migrant criminalization contributed to the social borderlands that overlaid the geographic border region and further shaped the religious landscape that my families' faith communities emerged from. Additionally, Borderlands Pentecostalism was shaped by vernacular Catholic practices, popular healing traditions, white leaders who relinquished power, and a cast of religious entrepreneurs. So while Bustos's "burned-over" imagery suggests a region of religiously exhausted residents, local innovation and migration to and through these borderlands contributed ongoing religious energy. My parents' families took part in the religious circulations that occurred in the borderlands.

Borderlands form the backdrop to this book as they deeply shape the Pentecostalism that my family has experienced. These borderlands encompass both the geopolitical realities of the US-Mexico border region and sociocultural dimensions of borderland life beyond border regions.[12] The work of Gloria Anzaldua has especially been pivotal in formulating borderlands as both geopolitical constructs and experiences of sociocultural liminality. Anzaldua famously described the US-Mexico borderlands as "una herida abierta where the Third World grates against the first and bleeds."[13] These borderlands are constructed through battles and wars, historical discourses, ongoing power differentials, and patterns of security, policing, and militarization. Inhabitants of said regions learn to move through the world in relation to these systems of power, with those on the edges of these regional societies often defying political boundaries.[14] Borderlands to some represent the vanguard of empire, where those most vulnerable confront the powers that be. Likewise, borderlands to some represent the edges of empire, where surviving populations, like Indigenous communities, labor migrants, and individuals dispossessed by nation states, continue to make lives for themselves. The Pentecostalism I came to know was largely shaped by people who navigated borderland realities on the margins.

The Pentecostal communities I grew up in reflected a sociocultural creativity characteristic of borderlands. Borderlands are often sites of cultural adaptation, where people of distinct backgrounds encounter each other, learn from each other, and forge new cultural expressions. In borderlands, peoples often forge third spaces—alternative spaces—that creatively counter the hierarchies and binaries along the border. The realities of Nepantla,[15] a state of liminality, are met with creative processes of community-building. Cultural innovation in the borderlands is not immune to hegemonic influences. Nevertheless, populations with less power find ways to adapt their own cultures, often through resistance, giving birth to new expressions of self in the face of violence and domination. As sociopolitical realities salient at borders are reproduced in locales throughout the nation, especially wherever powerful social boundaries impose distinct life outcomes on proximate populations, building alternative spaces becomes a labor of love and survival.

For borderland peoples on the margins, maintaining notions of self, agency, and dignity can be laborious, given that borderlands are spaces where memories are contested. At the borderlands, memories are often forgotten, reconfigured, or resurrected. Some borderland memories are laced with trauma; some people arrive at the borderlands fleeing trauma, and some experience trauma at the borderlands. As distinct national and economic regimes vie for power or maintain tenuous forms of stasis, borderlands uniquely absorb the brunt of these conflicts and exchanges, manifesting these retentions in living, breathing peoples and ecosystems. Peoples on the margins on both sides of the border are often left to construct, reconstruct, and resurrect aspects of their humanities that have been lost amid colonial legacies. The conflicting and contrasting narratives that orient notions of self and peoplehood in borderlands, alongside economic and political conditions, often force borderland people to reorient their relationships to their pasts.

The Spirit in the borderlands has assisted many in working to regain a sense of a whole and remembered self.[16] Here, the Spirit has been a source of strength, a sense of integrity and resilience, and grounds for placemaking and celebration amid ongoing change and brutal dislocation. Simultaneously, perhaps paradoxically, these communities of the Spirit are locales of adaptation that experience change themselves; in these processes of adaptation, especially amid conversion experiences, people release elements of their past selves. In some institutions, the Spirit is used as grounds for letting go. Here, I pose challenges to rupture practices that fast-track the erasure of memory for many Pentecostals. This work of the Spirit is, in some cases, a project of healing by letting go but in other cases might involve healing by retaining, reclaiming, and reinterpreting.

PENTECOSTALISM AS BORDERLAND SPACE

The beginnings of Pentecostalism reflect its borderland status as a movement on the margins of the proscriptive racial order[17] and as a movement that quickly expanded into the US-Mexico borderlands.[18] Scholars locate Pentecostalism's epicenter in Los Angeles, California, at the Azusa Street Revival of 1906. During this period, the ethnic Mexican population of Los Angeles was set to boom, with the population of peoples of Mexican origin expanding ten times, by some estimates,[19] in the decade following the revival's start. The Azusa Street Revival was held in a building that once housed an African Methodist Episcopalian church and was converted into a horse stable. Revival services initially took place seven days a week, typically three times a day.[20] A hallmark of the revival was its leader William Seymour's invitation for visitors to be baptized in the Holy Spirit, an experience of the spiritual seeker being empowered by God's presence and evidenced by speaking in tongues unknown to the speaker.

Seymour adapted his theology of the Holy Spirit to his experience of crossing social boundaries. The baptism in the Holy Spirit could be accompanied by additional miraculous acts, including healing and words of prophecy. This cosmology resonated with Seymour, who was raised in a region of Louisiana that was primarily Roman Catholic and was also known for practices of Afrodiasporic spiritualities. The very act of speaking in tongues signaled a crossing of linguistic borders, and potentially cultural and geographic borders, to share with others the gospel of Jesus Christ. Seymour embraced early Pentecostal theology after attending a Bible school in Houston, Texas, founded by Charles Parham. Due to Jim Crow laws, Seymour was only allowed to take classes by sitting outside the classroom.[21] He would go on to defy boundaries of race by preaching the Pentecostal message to diverse multitudes.

After accepting an invitation to pastor a church in Los Angeles, Seymour and his teachings about the baptism in the Holy Spirit and speaking in tongues were met with resistance at his new congregation. Though Seymour was ultimately barred from that church, some members and new acquaintances were interested in his teachings. Eventually, he gathered an interracial group of disciples who began meeting for fervent prayer at a home on Bonnie Brae Street. Diverse groups of onlookers were drawn to this spiritual spectacle as the prayer gatherings were hardly contained indoors. The site marked a precursor to the Azusa Street Revival as people there experienced baptisms in the Holy Spirit, including Seymour himself. Soon the group moved to a more spacious location, where they were able to share their experiences with others.

MEXICAN AND LATINO[22] PENTECOSTALS

When the revival meetings began at the building on Azusa Street, Mexicans were present. Mexican laborers were hired to alter the facility to accommodate revival visitors.[23] A group of Black American women from the Bonnie Brae prayer gathering also prepared the facility and held a time of prayer in anticipation of the services. One of these women began to testify to one of the Mexican workers. He ultimately broke down in tears and prayed to give his life to God. During the first week of revival services, an eyewitness claimed that a Mexican man with a clubfoot who attended the revival was healed and soon after received the baptism in the Holy Spirit. Mexicans were among the first to convert, the first to be healed, and the first to receive the baptism in the Holy Spirit, according to revival testimonies.

Reporter Frank Bartleman noted that "a man from the central part of Mexico, an Indian, was present in the meeting and heard a German sister speaking in his tongue which the Lord had given her."[24] According to Bartleman, in understanding the message, the Mexican man converted. After testifying, with the help of an interpreter, the Mexican Indian man prayed for a woman at the revival. The woman, "who was suffering from consumption,"[25] was instantly healed. Bartleman and the father of the woman healed referred to the Mexican Indian man as "rough" and "poor," respectively. As Ramirez points out, accounts of this man neglected details that would bring a sense of respect and dignity to his person. His social status as an Indigenous man likely positioned him in a subordinate status within the emerging social hierarchy of Los Angeles. His linguistic differences likely furthered his social marginalization. In contrast, the testimonies of Mexicans of more European descent were spotlighted in exemplary fashion; nevertheless, the presence of this Indigenous Mexican man signaled the possibilities of Mexican-origin peoples finding their place in Borderlands Pentecostalism.

In the end, Mexicans would be among those ordained by Rev. Seymour himself and were among those who traveled far and wide with the Pentecostal message. Various Mexican participants were included among those documented as having ties to the Azusa Street Revival:[26] Abundio and Rosa Lopez gained recognition for preaching in the Mexican Plaza district of downtown Los Angeles; day laborer Brigido Perez testified to receiving the baptism in the Holy Spirit at Azusa Street and traveled to San Diego to do evangelistic work there; Luís López, Juan Martínez Navarro, and Genaro and Romanita Carbajal Valenzuela circulated through the farm labor camps of Los Angeles and various surrounding counties, sharing the message they received at Azusa Street; Susie Villa Valdez maneuvered through the shanty towns of Los Angeles and beyond, sharing her message through song and word. Valdez's son, Adolfo, followed in his mother's footsteps, becoming one of the most prolific Pentecostal evangelists of his era, preaching across the United States and holding evangelistic meetings in Australia, New Zealand, India, China, and Japan. The Pentecostal communities that emerged through these early efforts were often binational and cross-border in nature. The ties of cultural exchange, communication, and spiritual camaraderie ensured that early Pentecostalism was a borderland movement.[27]

Borderland Convergence

Ultimately, the Pentecostal message reached the borderland regions that my parents were from, and my parents' families came into contact with the Pentecostal message. My father, Alvaro Calvillo, encountered Pentecostalism in Ciudad Juárez, Chihuahua; my mother in Tijuana, Baja California. They would both be socialized into the Pentecostal networks of the Assemblies of God, learning about numerous churches throughout their respective regions and being exposed to preaching and music from pastors, evangelists, and musicians in the region. When their respective families migrated to California, the families converged within a small church in the barrio borderlands of Fullerton.

The little barrio church, Templo El Buen Pastor,[28] was located in a Mexican neighborhood formed in an era when many of Orange County's Mexican households were segregated within identifiable *colonias*. In a previous century, working-class Mexicans faced stark segregation from whites, as described by local reporter Emerson Little: "According to old Fullerton planning commission minutes, back in 1915, residents insisted that the city's police department block Mexicans from leaving their houses after an outbreak of scarlet fever. Four years later, hundreds of residents protested at a city council meeting after they learned that the Santa Fe Railroad planned to build housing for its Mexican workers near the company's tracks."[29]

One of the earliest housing desegregation cases, in fact, took place in Fullerton, California. Through the Superior Court proceedings of *Doss et al. v. Bernal et al.*, 1923 segregationist housing-deed restrictions against Mexican Americans were declared unconstitutional, setting a precedent. Not much later, in another part of Orange County, *Mendez v. Westminster* struck down the legal segregation of Mexican school children. These victories meant that, decades later, families like mine could build lives in other parts of the city. Nevertheless, the barrio, and the barrio church, remained a place of connection.

It was into a barrio church, to a Pentecostal preacher woman, that I was born. The cadence, the enunciation, the enlivened pronouncements and punctuated pauses came to me through the womb. I imagine my heartbeat absorbed and synchronized with the rhythm of my mother's vocalizations before I could form a vivid memory. Still, some of my earliest memories are of my mother, Lydia, speaking from the pulpit. As a child, I was allowed to take a pillow to church and would fall asleep under the pews. The syncopated lilt of orators and the groans of spiritual seekers at the altar lulled me to sleep. Yet it was my mother's preaching that first resonated with me as she would invite the Holy Spirit to minister to the congregation. These were the moments in which she preached impassioned sermons or methodically taught lessons during adult Sunday school classes. Her desire to see others live their lives in fullness permeated her speech. I have yet to escape the resonance that I experienced in this early sanctuary. It was a call to come forward and experience the Spirit within sanctuaries of subaltern agency and creativity. Borderlands Pentecostalism has been with me from the start.

INTERSECTING BORDERLANDS

This book is about how members of my family and I encountered the Holy Spirit as the Spirit *en la frontera* and experienced Pentecostalism as a faith forged in the borderlands. The lived religious practices that we adapted and enacted in the spaces we moved through and inhabited[30] were largely developed within a borderlands context and addressed borderland realities of cultural convergence, power differentials, and racialization. These lived religious practices manifested within and beyond the walls of traditional institutions. Through these pages, I spotlight how in the Borderlands Pentecostalism of my peoples, the Spirit has been known as God active since the dawn of creation, guiding a downtrodden people to freedom, disassembling walls of division, nurturing creative gifts in people, and cultivating communities of healing. The Spirit both crosses borders and inhabits *fronteras*, or borderlands. There are moments of finality and completion in the Spirit and moments of waiting and liminality in the Spirit.

The flow of the book tracks encounters with the Spirit *en la frontera* as mediated by the Pentecostalism of my community. The book of Acts in the Christian Scriptures depicts how the Holy Spirit energized followers of Jesus Christ as they crossed social boundaries of ethnicity, race, class, gender, and citizenship to dispense the very same liberating Spirit they claimed to have encountered. Many of my family members saw themselves as heirs of this spiritual lineage.[31] Though the spread of Christianity has been intertwined with empire, it has often been in marginalized populations and through forced diasporas that versions of Christianity such as Pentecostalism have taken root and taken on lives of their own.[32] Undoubtedly, Pentecostalism itself has had to grapple with its relationship to empire. Nevertheless, for many of the Latino Pentecostals whom I encountered throughout my life, crossing borders, social and geopolitical, was a matter of survival, and as these Pentecostals crossed, the Spirit crossed with them. This Spirit was not beholden to empire but rather empowered peoples on the margins to make a way in the face of empire. I attempt to capture here that Spirit *en las fronteras*, for the many borders traversed through my own lifeworlds.

I begin by spotlighting the forms of creative agency that Pentecostals exercised in order to maintain a sense of personhood and a collective sense of peoplehood amid borderland realities. In my formative years, I was especially shaped by the practices of performance and creativity that Pentecostals engaged in. I then move into particular rites of passage that I encountered in my Borderlands Pentecostal world. These rites combine formal institutional components and informal expressions of lived religion. Finally, I describe the continued mobilities that I navigated in relation to the Pentecostal communities that shaped me. I consider how the resonances of a prior generation of Pentecostalism continue to be reimagined within new contexts toward developing strategies of survival and resilience in my own life.

CULTIVATIONS

I set the tone for the rest of this journey by remembering another one of my Pentecostal forebears, my maternal grandmother, Nana Josefina. One of the ways my grandmother laid down roots in Fullerton, California, after migrating from her native region of Sonora, Mexico, was through gardening. The plants she cultivated set their roots in the California borderland soils around her. During my childhood, Nana lived across the street from my parents' home, and my brother David and I interacted with her daily. For many of those years, she gardened in my parents' backyard, creating a lush landscape in a small walled-in space that was the scene of many an adventure for my childhood action figures. Among the trees she planted, one remains today: a citrus tree. A unique aspect of this tree is that, through my grandmother's engraftation skills, it bears two kinds of citrus fruits: sweet lime and bitter lemon. Like the engrafted portion of this tree, my ancestors were not always tied to Pentecostalism, but this was the community they engrafted onto in the borderlands. The roots may not be the original source of the engrafted branches, but the branching out has drawn important nourishment from this source for several generations. This book connects the ever-expanding borderland branches I encounter today to the borderland roots I was engrafted upon.

PART ONE

Finding Our Way

CHAPTER ONE

Creative Circulations within Congregations

The creativity that migrants exercise and encounter through their migrations has helped strengthen communal identities across geographies and generations in Borderlands Pentecostalism. Such was the discovery of two young men who visited El Buen Pastor Church in Fullerton, California, for the first time. The two travelers visiting the small barrio church received a warm welcome that Sunday morning in the mid-1970s. These brothers, Arturo and Ismael, had circulated through the US borderlands as labor migrants, alongside parents and siblings, going as far as Northern California before stopping back in Los Angeles. The family originally planned to return to the El Paso–Juarez region. With members of the household having spent the last several years living and doing odd jobs in Texas, New Mexico, and California, and some siblings settling at different points along this migratory circuit, the hope of having everyone back together in Juarez or El Paso was fading. At the time, the family was living at a church in East Los Angeles that they attended on a previous migration journey, but they sensed impermanence there. So that morning in Fullerton, the smiles, conversations, hearty handshakes, and questions about their well-being felt like home to the young men. Soon, their creative gifts would further connect them to the church.

Arturo and Ismael Calvillo, my uncles, drove across California county lines that day to reconnect with an old friend. Their friend, Samuel, had migrated from Ciudad Juárez to Fullerton, in Orange County, neighboring Los Angeles County. Samuel attended Templo El Buen Pastor and invited my uncles to visit him there. My uncle Ismael, known as Mayel, brought his guitar with him and carried borderland songs within him. After the church service, my uncle played the guitar and sang *coritos* he'd learned in El Paso and Juarez. My uncle's music caught the attention of church regular Hermano Ramirez. These songs that had circulated through the borderland circuits included some of Hermano Ramirez's favorites. When he learned that my uncles' current housing situation was tenuous, Hermano Ramirez offered them a place to stay at a nearby property he owned. After the brothers went back to Los Angeles and deliberated with family, the Calvillo family made the decision to move to this new home. This rental agreement signed with musical notes became the family's entry point into Orange County. They would fill this new home with music.

The Spirit in Borderlands Pentecostalism is characterized by creative movement across geographies and generations. In the borderlands, strategies of survival and sustainability among residents and sojourners often involve negotiating ties to multiple geographies and generations; the negotiations that take place across these dimensions are reflected in the creative representations within these communities such as music, poetry, oratory traditions, theater, and humor. Indeed, creative representations are sites of negotiation, and distinct cohorts of borderland peoples seek to express their authentic selves through creative acts. In the two churches where I grew up, El Buen Pastor and Las Buenas Nuevas, and in the dozens of Borderlands Pentecostal churches I visited in my early years, I observed the constant negotiation of geographic and generational differences. Yet, even as these negotiations sometimes moved toward routinization and standardization, they were largely characterized by movement and change. As new generational and geographic cohorts arrived within new church contexts, they added to the creative wealth of each particular community. Thus, even as trends in the organizational field influenced church expressions toward assimilatory US practices, these churches engaged in vibrant negotiations rooted in internal diversity.

AN INTERGENERATIONAL
CONGREGATION: EL BUEN PASTOR

An elderly woman in a fancy hat, gloves, and elegant dress closed her poem with poise and style: "Y mil rosas dejo ante tus pies" ["And a thousand roses I leave at your feet"]. Her wavering voice was overshadowed by the unwavering conviction of her words. Her poem recitation was worship unto God. Her couplets had filled the sanctuary of the church, a space that seated a little over a hundred people. The small chapel building was adjoined by several classrooms, a handful of parking spots in the back, and a patch of green lawn in the front. The place seemed huge to me. It was around 1982, and I was about four years old. The presence of this woman—Hermana Taide, as we knew her—in that moment was larger than life.

That day, I asked my mother what all that had been about. I still remember the ending of the poem because my mother repeated it as she explained the poem's meaning. Hermana Taide was one of the mainstays of the congregation at Templo El Buen Pastor. She was part of a particular migration cohort to the community. The fact that the church allowed her to share her gift of poetry was special. Her creativity in writing and recitation left an impression on me. She represented an older generation of congregants that now sustained that small barrio church through their creative acts. She helped generate the culture that welcomed subsequent generations of migrants to the church, bringing their own creative elements to the community. In this way, El Buen Pastor formed part of a larger ethnic and migrant circuit of creative exchange characteristic of Borderlands Pentecostalism, wherein ethnic creativity was continually replenished.[1]

My mother's family joined El Buen Pastor after circulating through the borderlands as well. The family faced generational economic instability following the Mexican Revolution and labored in a variety of trades. My mother's family circulated along the US-Mexico border, for years moving between towns in Sonora, Mexico; Baja California, Mexico; and eventually Arizona and California. My maternal Sanchez-Fraijo side of the family arrived in Fullerton several years prior to the Calvillo family's arrival. My mother and her sister Sara came to California from Arizona following in the footsteps of their oldest sister, Yolanda, who worked at a manufacturing plant in Los Angeles County. Economic and household dynamics influenced my mother and her sisters to migrate. In this season, my grandparents separated. My mother and her sisters helped my grandmother Josefina Fraijo migrate to Fullerton, where she could start over. This was a migration led by women creating sustainable lives. The Sanchez sisters worked to support their mother and each other, living in a small apartment in the old Fullerton barrio. My mother initially worked a manufacturing job in Compton, California. The church served as a source of social support for the sisters.[2] My grandmother Josefina stayed in Fullerton for the rest of her life, the matriarch of a growing, extended family.

When my mother's family arrived at El Buen Pastor, the congregation was undergoing significant demographic shifts. It was a Latino Pentecostal church affiliated with the Assemblies of God Latino District.[3] At the time, many of the earlier congregants were Chicanos.[4] In the 1970s, the old Mexican barrio where the church was located had a substantial native-born population. The congregation reflected these demographics. Many Chicano congregants were bilingual, but their dominant language was English. Some were *pochos*,[5] and their Spanish was *mocho*.[6] Linguistic negotiations have long been a part of Borderlands Pentecostalism, and at El Buen Pastor, linguistic negotiations in the 1970s were largely tied to generational cohort differences. As my mother and father's families converged within El Buen Pastor, they formed part of a cohort of newer immigrants coming from Southwest borderland regions; most of them were Spanish-dominant, and they began to interact with local English-speaking Chicanos.

The intergenerational convergence at El Buen Pastor prompted distinct cohorts to build solidarity together through creativity. My parents recall the oratory skills of one of the pastors, who was Chicano, as he attempted to preach in Spanish, catering to more newly arrived Spanish speakers. This pastor, Rev. Camarillo, at times struggled to recall certain Spanish words. For example, he once struggled to say the Spanish word for statue, *estatua*, repeatedly pronouncing it "es-tua-ta." After the service ended, he walked to the front entrance of the church, facing the neighborhood street, and yelled out "*estatua!*" this time correctly pronouncing the word. On another occasion, he struggled to pronounce the Spanish word for "in love," *enamorado*. Throughout his sermon, he pronounced it "e-ne-mo-rado." He was visibly bothered by his slight mispronunciation as he detected his own error. Again, once the service ended, he walked to the front entrance of the church and yelled out, "In love!" Stories such as these lived on in the church lore, as members accommodated each other's linguistic capacities.

My parents' migration cohorts brought creative linguistic practices of their own to the congregation. One particular incident recalled by my parents illustrates the linguistic transitions taking place in the congregational setting: On one occasion, as my father and uncles participated in one of the youth Bible studies, members laughed as my teenage uncle was berated by the Sunday school leaders for speaking in slang. He had used the word *agüitado* to express that he felt sad. He was told to use proper Spanish. He responded, "Pues como digo que me siento agüitado?" ["How should I say that I'm feeling blue?"] His friend attempted to help: "Pues que te sientes colgado" ["Well, tell them you feel droopy"]. The youth group burst into laughter as the friend used one slang term to replace another. The church became an institution that attempted to rein in these young men even as they infused the church with their creative linguistics.[7]

One of the influences present in the borderlands that the church community had to contend with was pachuquismo, or pachuco culture, which was intermingled with the borderlands' youth culture of the time. The word *agüitado*, for example, comes from pachuco culture. Pachuquismo's roots are in the borderland circuits of cultural exchange traversed by migrants and the rural and urban working class. My father and his siblings grew up in the cradle of pachuquismo, the twin-city region of Ciudad Juárez, Chihuahua, Mexico, bordering El Paso, Texas, a city known as El Pachuco.[8] Caló was the argot he and his peers communicated in. Pachuquismo had spread in the earlier twentieth century from borderland communities in El Paso and along the rail lines that many young Chicanos worked on, all the way to Los Angeles.

My mother also influenced the linguistic expressions of El Buen Pastor through her preaching. She learned to preach while enrolled at a Bible institute in Tijuana, Mexico, starting at the age of thirteen. As she was lacking the opportunity for secondary education in her hometown, the chance to attend a denominational Bible school was promising. By then, my mother was Pentecostal and had become affiliated with the Assemblies of God. At Instituto Bíblico Betania de las Asambleas de Dios,[9] she received theological training, alongside other ministers in training. While training to be a minister and an evangelist, she excelled at preaching.

During and after Bible school, my mother spent time helping the denomination conduct evangelistic gatherings and establish new churches throughout Mexico, with a brief stint in Central America. Though my mother had traveled expansive circuits through her training and ministry, the move to California was different. She was in her late twenties and had given over a decade of her life to the work of the church. The growing Pentecostal church network in California offered new prospects. The little church in Fullerton, indeed, offered opportunities for my mother to activate her ministry gifts. In the mid-1970s, my mother began to teach and preach at the church. She became the director of the youth ministry there and taught young adult Sunday school to a growing community of teen and young adult learners. Her gifts of preaching and teaching became blessings to the little barrio church, as preaching was an art for her.

CONGREGATIONAL SONGS

"El Hermanito Jonathan tiene un canto para compartir con nosotros esta mañana" ["Little brother Jonathan has a song to share with us this morning"]. My mother was startled by the words she heard from the pastor. She looked up to discover that I was standing on the stage, microphone in hand, ready to sing a song: "Tomado de la mano, yo voy / Tomado de la mano, yo voy!" I began to sing accompanied by the church musicians. During the offering time, I had escaped my mother's watch. We typically sat toward the front of the church. I felt comfortable approaching the pastor and requesting to sing a song. The pastor accepted my request. I was only three years old, and this happened several times. On all occasions, the song I sang was "Tomado de la Mano," about holding Jesus's hand and following him wherever he went.

The song was familiar to me as we regularly sang it at church. My family also had a record of the song at home, as recorded by Christian singer Manuel Bonilla. The first recording I was able to identify was from 1978, an arrangement by Rafael Espinoza, recorded by Grupo de Sinaloa, an Apostolic Pentecostal musical group based in Sinaloa, Mexico. That year, 1978, was also the year I was born. The song had made its way through the Pentecostal circuits and landed in Southern California, crossing over between oneness Pentecostals and trinitarian Pentecostals. It was likely composed long before the 1978 recording. Borderland songs had made their way into my repertoire and shaped my practices through these creative borderland circuits.

In the 1970s and early 1980s, borderlands hymnody had migrated throughout the Southwest and had gained familiarity across geographic and generational groups. The hymnody of my Pentecostal church reflected the layers of ethnic community and migratory routes that crisscrossed the local community.[10] Many of the songs that were sung at church were *coritos*, short choruses that could be strung together as a medley and were often accompanied by a guitar. I recall how these faster, celebratory songs energized the congregation. Often, the rattling of tambourines accompanied these songs, adding a fuller polyrhythm to the impromptu arrangements. The worship leaders strung together the songs of their choice, calling out the name of a song before it began. Church regulars were ready for the switch-up and followed along seamlessly.

One of the best-known *coritos* is "Alabare," a song that has crossed regional and denominational borders.[11] My parents have sung it since their early years in Pentecostalism, and some of my earliest memories involve singing it. "Alabare" illustrates how Pentecostal hymnody drew from a wide range of sources. The origins of the song are difficult to pinpoint, in part because of its widespread use and adaptation. A number of traditions adopted it and adapted it, making it their own, decades ago. Some copyright documentation of the song suggests it had Catholic origins, attributing it to Spanish composers Jose Pagan and Manuel Jose Alonso in 1979.[12] Nevertheless, Baptist minister Roberto Savage published the song in a Puerto Rican hymnal in 1973,[13] listing 1952 as the composition date, which suggests a different origin. Either the song originated with the Baptists, or it had crossed over into Baptist hymnody by the 1950s. This also suggests a Puerto Rican origin to the song, signaling how Protestant hymnody migrated beyond ethno-nationalist and denominational lines.[14]

Congregational songs represented an array of aesthetic stylings. Some captured an aesthetic resembling boleros, slower and more melancholy. I think of the old song "Amarte Solo a Ti, Señor," which speaks of a focused devotion to God and letting go of the past. Recorded versions of the song often featured harmonizing and smooth, lilting vocalizations. Other songs carried a cumbia rhythm, such as "Alla en el Monte Horeb." As was sung in my church, it carried a swing that worshippers could not help but sway to. The song spoke of when Moses encountered the burning bush and had to remove his shoes as he was on holy ground. Many songs included motifs from the Hebrew Scriptures and attempted to capture a Jewish sonic registry; this often included usage of what music theorists describe as the augmented second, a dropping down of the second note, below the major keys. The song "O Jerusalén," pining for a future abode in the New Jerusalem while connoting nostalgia for the present Jerusalem, draws on this augmented second-pattern characteristic of Jewish music.

Finally, El Buen Pastor frequently drew on traditional hymns within its worship services. As the church was affiliated with the Assemblies of God, it used *Himnos de Gloria*,[15] the hymnal most used by the denomination. Many hymns were translated from English hymns, though most congregants knew them only in Spanish. Some Spanish-language hymns did make it into the hymnal, however.

The combination of hymns and *coritos* marked an important contrast within Pentecostal hymnody and ritual in that era. On the one hand, there was a desire to retain a statelier and more traditional practice of worship, namely the singing of hymns. Hymns were sung with solemnity and reverence. Even joyful hymns drew people into a more rigid corporeal stance as compared with *coritos*. *Coritos*, however, provided an opportunity to let loose. Here, people might raise their hands, sway, clap, and express deep emotions. Shouts of "aleluyah" and "gloria Adios" erupted during *coritos*.[16] There were typically times designated to sing hymns and others to sing *coritos*. Hymns were good openers, a way to draw people into focus and to contemplate a particular spiritual truth contained in the hymns' lyrics. *Coritos* were a time to seek an unpredictable encounter with the Spirit.

CONGREGATIONAL MOVEMENTS

Creative movements occurred even when migrants settled into regions long term, as congregants often transferred across local congregations. When I was about five years old, my family joined Las Buenas Nuevas, another congregation in our denomination. This was also a barrio church, in the predominantly Latine city of Norwalk, California, on the eastern edge of Los Angeles County. Freeway close, the church drew a commuter population spread throughout the greater Los Angeles area. The congregation there was more diverse than the congregation at El Buen Pastor. During the 1980s, I established friendships with peers who represented a full spectrum of Latin American and Caribbean origin groups.

At Las Buenas Nuevas, a fullness of Latinidad had converged. Latinidad is the notion that peoples of Latin American and Spanish-speaking Caribbean descent share substantial cultural similarities and histories, and by extension, their experiences and social locations in the US context are mutually intelligible despite their differences. My sense of being Latino developed at Las Buenas Nuevas. Similar to El Buen Pastor, Las Buenas Nuevas retained a remnant of Chicanos

from the region, reflecting the local Chicano population from surrounding communities. Yet different cohorts of migration throughout the Los Angeles basin had diversified this congregation. During
my childhood years there, I grew up visiting the homes of friends of
Guatemalan, Nicaraguan, Salvadoran, Puerto Rican, Dominican,
and other national origins.

My church relationships provided me with a cultural repository
and a sense of panethnic belonging at an important juncture in my
educational journey. In the third grade, I was admitted into a program for "gifted" students. I was transferred from my Latine-majority
elementary school to a program with few other Latine students; I was
the only Latine student in my grade who was there for all four years
of the program. Most of the classmates I established friendships with
were white and Asian American. With few Latine peers at school,
my church connections provided important access to Latine peers
outside of my family. Though in recent years important critiques of
Latinidad have circulated,[17] particularly offering correctives to the
anti-Blackness and anti-indigeneity pervasive in Latinidad, notions
of Latinidad influenced the support systems within my congregation. The trust networks[18] that were established among congregants
assumed we could understand each other and learn from each other;
the practices of shared faith especially energized these ties. I observed
similar patterns at other churches that we visited. My sense of being
Mexican American *and* Latino became salient because of my participation at church.

Despite the diversity of the congregational makeup, the worship
practices at Las Buenas Nuevas reflected a proper and respectable
classic Pentecostalism; this Pentecostalism leaned into traditions
formalized in the Southwest and in other pockets of Mexican migration throughout the United States. In our years there, Las Buenas
Nuevas was led by Mexican American pastors well recognized in
our denomination. The repertoires of Latino Pentecostalism that
these leaders reflected emerged in a time when Pentecostals were
highly marginalized and when peoples of Mexican origin struggled
to gain acceptance in US society. Many had worked strenuously to

succeed. I think, for example, of one of our pastors, Rev. Dr. Dean Gonzalez, born in Wyoming to Mexican American parents who were farm laborers; he went on to earn a PhD. His wife, Hermana Tillie, came from a Texas-based family who worked in agriculture; she was a gifted pianist, among other things. The two embodied a refined image of respectability.

In this context, more effusive hallmarks of Pentecostalism were counterbalanced by restrained expressions of worship and personal presentation. Our music, for example, largely relied on a single piano player and, outside of special events, had no drums, guitars, or other instruments. *Panderos*, or tambourines, were present but used sparingly at church services. On Sundays, we sang hymns from hymnals, subdued contemporary songs, and a few *coritos*. Special numbers were usually sung to cassette instrumentals and rarely had a strong beat, though some of the vocalists displayed their broad vocal ranges.

Latin American and Caribbean diversity often showed up through lived religious expressions and through special occasions. For example, the accents reflected in the occasional call and response revealed the array of backgrounds present in the congregation. I distinctly remember, for instance, the voice of an elderly Puerto Rican *hermana* who called out, "Santo!" at high points in the service. Moments of praying out loud also accented the diversity in our midst. One of my favorite church weddings featured a Christian salsa band, although we were not allowed to dance. Guest preachers and guest singers significantly broadened the front-stage representation from throughout Latin America and the Caribbean. Evangelists such as Dina Santamaria from El Salvador and Josue Yrion from Brazil were among the favorites of the congregation. Likewise, in theatrical performances, people of disparate backgrounds shared the stage. During Christmastime, congregants infused aspects of their cultural expressions from throughout Latin America and the Caribbean into the imagined scenes of Bethlehem and Jerusalem created in our barrio church. As I participated in these dramatizations from a young age, I experienced the camaraderie of these productions.

BORDERLANDS CONSCIOUSNESS

Homeland visits shaped the creative borderlands consciousness of families like mine. When we visited family in San Luis, Arizona, or El Paso, Texas, we visited churches on both sides of the border. In those years, I observed how many churchgoing *fronterizos* built spiritual community across borders.[19] Some of my family members lived in the United States and attended church in Mexico. While it was more difficult for people from Mexico to attend church in the United States, many congregants in Mexico maintained ties to US churches through family and denominational relations. Furthermore, for me, traveling to Mexico meant visiting churches in Mexico. I remember attending Sunday school classes with children in Mexico, worshipping in Mexican church sanctuaries, and being introduced to pastors and leaders in Mexico. Despite being born in the United States, I understood my faith as being linked to people on the other side of the US-Mexico border. I also knew I was privileged to travel outside of the United States as not all congregants could. Yet, like my family, other households traveled back to their homelands, allowing young people to experience homeland faith communities.

My creative borderlands imagination especially expanded when my family and I traveled to Mexico City and Veracruz, Mexico. Dear family friends Lolita and Juan Martinez and their children, of Veracruz, Mexico, prompted our visit to that region. They were friends of my parents as my mother had attended Bible institute with Rev. Lolita. Pastors Lolita and Juan led a church in the historic port city of Veracruz. They annually visited family in California and often stayed with us. The Martinez family were kin to us, with the children calling my parents *Tio* and *Tia*. After my father gained US residency status and was able to travel by plane, we arranged a trip to Veracruz for the first time; this was also our first time flying as a family.

I was fifteen years old and was introduced to aspects of Mexican culture that I had little knowledge of previously. In Veracruz, I learned about peoples of African descent in Mexico. The port of Veracruz is where many enslaved Africans were first brought to Mexico. When there, we visited the sixteenth-century fort of San Juan de Ulua, a critical site of intercontinental trade across the Americas, Europe, and Asia; it was recently declared a UNESCO site of memory, especially recognizing that it was built by enslaved peoples of African descent. The state of Veracruz is home to Afro-Mexican communities that have historically overcome discrimination and marginalization and yet have significantly influenced the broader Mexican population.

In Veracruz, I learned about son jarocho, the regional music that developed with the convergence of African, European, and Indigenous peoples.[20] The song "La Bamba," I learned, was originally a son jarocho tune that developed into a multitude of verses composed at festive occasions, perhaps as early as the seventeenth century. The name *bamba*, by some accounts, is of African etymology. When visiting church with the Martinez family, I absorbed the ways the local culture was represented in worship, particularly through the music and preaching. Later in that trip, we traveled to Mexico City and visited the expansive pyramid ruins of San Juan de Teotihuacan as well as the *Zócalo* in Mexico City. Gaining knowledge of Mexican history and culture under the guidance of the Martinez family expanded my understanding of what it meant to be Mexican American and Latino. I began to feel an ethnic pride that I had never experienced before. That fall, at the start of my sophomore year in high school, I wore an Aztec medallion that I had purchased in Mexico.

THE INFLUENCES OF MIGRATION

In 1994, when I was sixteen years old, my family and I rejoined El Buen Pastor church. Through prayerful consideration, my parents saw an opportunity to help our old church as it had undergone a division in recent years and was rebuilding. My parents, who were respected lay church leaders, were valued for their potential in helping to rebuild the church. By then, the church itself had relocated to a new facility, not far from the small barrio chapel where it previously met. Church leaders had purchased a building that was formerly a gun shop, equipped with several shooting ranges downstairs. The new building provided more classrooms and office space.

The church had also significantly changed demographically during the decade that we were gone. The congregation had diversified, especially with newer members who had come from Central America and the Caribbean. The pastors, Gladys and Quintin Lazaro, were Peruvian. Quietly, they committed themselves to building up young leaders within the church as well as helping long-standing members heal from the church division. We noted a sense of grief that was prevalent in the church community in that first season back, and this was my first experience of collective mourning over institutional disagreements.

Unlike the more formal and traditional forms of church worship prevalent at Las Buenas Nuevas, the new El Buen Pastor drew on worship forms that reflected the broader tastes of the community. The rhythms of cumbia, salsa, and *norteñas* made their way through Sunday morning services. Even though the church had gone through a season of sadness, the musical expressions were a space for joy. Here, the worship teams at various points included Cuban, Puerto Rican, and Salvadoran musicians, alongside Mexican, Guatemalan, Costa Rican, and Nicaraguan singers. The musical repertoire often drew from the Latin American contemporary worship music movement, including music from composers such as Marcos Witt, Jesus Adrian Romero, and Juan Carlos Alvarado. Worship expressions were at times less polished as newer musicians and singers were allowed to develop their gifts publicly, but that was part of the "can-do" rebuilding spirit of the church.

Migration was influencing the congregational worship preferences in the greater Los Angeles area in our congregation. Movements such as Elim and Llamada Final,[21] for example, regionally popularized a style of worship that purported to reflect Jewish aesthetics and Old Testament symbolism. This style of worship was often accompanied by liturgical dance, including both choreographed and impromptu expressions from congregants. Tambourines, flags, and shofar horns were among the paraphernalia that surfaced within this worship style. The movements were especially prevalent in communities that had significant Central American representation. In the 1990s, this style of worship caught on like wildfire. El Buen Pastor reflected a tempered version of these worship aesthetics, borrowing some of the songs popular in this movement but being cautious about liturgical dance. Some members of the worship team were drawn to this style and visited churches that employed it. The influences would show up in our worship services.

Creative circulations increasingly brought congregants in touch with diverging theologies. This pattern led to church debates over doctrine, especially prosperity gospel theology. The language of word-of-faith and prosperity gospel theology was becoming prevalent in many Latino Pentecostal spaces. Some of our in-house lay preachers exhorted the church members to bring their prayer requests before God in faith. One in-house preacher, for example, once stated that to say, "If this is your will, Lord" when praying for healing or for another divine intervention demonstrated a lack of faith. The preacher insisted that if we knew something was God's will, we should declare it as such. An insistence that God wanted to bless his people was also part of this message.

While prosperity preaching is often criticized as benefiting wealthy preachers, I typically witnessed these messages coming from working-class peoples on the margins.[22] These declarations and understandings of a God that responds to the faith of believers represented an empowering message to some of those I knew. Yet the message was not for everyone, and some preferred to embrace a life of hope that waited on God with patience or that acknowledged the struggles they faced. I recall, for example, one incident when two congregants, both of them immigrants, prayed at the altar together out loud. One of the congregants, a university student engaged in social actions for racial equality, mourned that California had shot down affirmative action within its state schools. The other congregant prayed with fervor and celebrated that God had made him more than a conqueror. One cried, "Perdimos, Señor!"[23] while the other declared, "Tenemos victoria en Jesucristo."[24] The latter congregant later testified to having recently read a book written by a faith preacher. This juxtaposition, of the mourning congregant who had not gotten the results he arduously organized for and the congregant who declared victory over his own life, represented a borderlands reality. The borderlands church was a space in which people hoped for hope while at the same time wrestling with day-to-day struggles of inequality. These realities coexisted, and congregants worked creatively to understand the distinct theodicies embodied by their church peers.

CONNECTING CIRCUITS

The Spirit in Borderlands Pentecostalism was characterized by the creative expressions that permeated the expansive migratory circuits I encountered. The generational negotiations that ensued in these communities were influenced by the distinct migratory cohorts who arrived at the church. Creative expressions that came to dominate often reflected the tastes and preferences of the cohorts with the most influence. Given these cross-cultural negotiations in a pan-ethnic context, congregants exercised creativity to better accommodate their peers. Circulations within the region and across borders provided continual flows of cultural resources. These continued flows of creativity spanned geographies and generations even when agreements were difficult to achieve. Often, creativity functioned as the currency that helped people work together across differences to generate expressions that brought them into an experience of the Spirit. The Spirit *en las fronteras* moved through these creative acts.

CHAPTER TWO

To Be a Testimonio

As my father backed a car out of the family driveway in Ciudad Juárez, he was dismayed to discover his two younger sisters playing behind the vehicle. Stepping on the brake pedal, he was horrified to find that the brakes gave out. The car continued in reverse, severely injuring one of the girls. My tia Nena was told by hospital doctors that she would not walk again without assistance. The family was devastated. My grandmother Ama had heard about Pentecostalism from her sister, Hermila. Hermila suggested that Ama take Nena to the local Pentecostal church to be prayed for. Ama, Tia Nena, and several other family members accepted Hermila's advice and visited La Trinidad church, an Assemblies of God congregation in Ciudad Juárez, Mexico. There, Tia Nena was prayed for. As the testimonio goes, she was healed and soon after resumed her full physical activities. Several family members prayed to give their lives to Jesus Christ at that church. My father started to attend as well and accepted the gospel message they preached and the Pentecostal perspectives they taught. Soon, church gatherings were taking place at the Calvillo home. This was a family testimonio from the mid-1960s.

The word and concept *testimonio*, in my communities of upbringing, carried with it a weightiness. *Testimonios*, the Spanish cognate of *testimonies*, show up in many forms of Christianity. In Borderlands Pentecostal churches, *testimonios* are an art form and merit their own category of practice and meaning distinct from the broader concept of testimonies. Testimonios have been a central part of Latino Pentecostal life from the beginning. According to one eyewitness of the Azusa Street Revival, Frank Bartleman,[1] Mexicans who attended the revival were eager to testify about their faith. Since then, the practice of testimonios has flourished within Borderlands Pentecostal churches and remains a hallmark of Pentecostal practice. Testimonios were a way to understand one's place in the world as Pentecostal Christians and one's place in the community. To be a Borderlands Pentecostal was to *have* and *be* a testimonio.

HAVING A TESTIMONIO, BEING A TESTIMONIO

Testimonios, storytelling about self, kin, and community, are a means of self-making, a way of situating oneself in the world and articulating where one belongs. As narrative projections of one's self, testimonios encapsulate the aspects of one's life that are most meaningful or virtuous, that demarcate one's most salient identities, and/or that denote significant events or processes of identity formation. Certainly, in Christian traditions, testimonios articulate the work of God in the life of the believer, but they are not merely generic stories about God; these are deeply personal firsthand accounts. For Latino Pentecostals, testimonios are stories of encounters with God, of revelations from God, of miracles—both mundane and momentous—that remind believers they are not alone. For Borderlands Pentecostals, testimonios are largely about encountering Jesus Christ in the borderlands.

To be a self, an agentic being, in the Latino Pentecostal community is to have a testimonio and to be a testimonio. People have testimonies as they honor encounters now past. These stories become codified, scripturalized,[2] with retellings mirroring accounts from the early Christians in the New Testament Scriptures or from figures in the Hebrew Scriptures.[3] The form testimonies take is influenced by the testifier's church affiliation[4] and the particular themes or "narrative plots" that these institutions emphasize.[5] Yet *testimonio* also connotes action. Testificando, or testifying, is one way to be a testimony. To *testificar* is to invite others into one's own story. This entails the practice of sharing one's testimonio in a public manner. It is an act of encouraging others and of participating in the Spirit moving in the moment. Giving testimonio also points to everyday living. To *dar buen testimonio* [give a good testimony] was to live a good Christian life. A person who gave a bad testimonio was seen as being duplicitous, as being inconsistent in who they claimed to be and how they actually lived. Thus, testimonios needed to be protected. I recall the admonitions of church elders to "guarda tu testimonio" ["guard your testimony"]. These words might be used to encourage someone floundering or to coax someone into action. Nevertheless, they highlight that a testimonio is something living, to be nurtured and nourished.

The ongoing aspects of testimonio practices highlight the living nature of testimonios. Testimonios, as narratives, often conclude with some type of resolution, pointing to a finished act. And yet, when considered cumulatively, a person's testimonio is more of an ongoing dialogue with God and community. In this ongoing dialogue, testimonios often meet mundane needs. These are opportunities to share information and request assistance. While testimonios are presented as a finished product, the people sharing them are works in progress, and testimonios often highlight where that work requires intervention.

TESTIMONIOS IN CONTEXT

In the churches where I grew up, testimonios were delivered in several different ways. Many testimonio practices were developed within church services, a key site of testimonio delivery and socialization. Some services had entire segments dedicated to testimonios, where congregants could volunteer in impromptu fashion to come forward and share personal stories. This was not a typical Sunday morning occurrence but was common at weekday or Sunday evening services. In more formal, structured services, there might be a time designated for a specific person to come forward and share a special testimonio. Sometimes, after especially thrilling services that had extended times at the altar, someone might be given space to share about a breakthrough they experienced at the altar. Preachers also embedded testimonios within their sermons, sharing their own stories of spiritual victory.

I grew up hearing testimonios shared by family at home and at extended family gatherings, not solely at church gatherings. The testimonio format was often a way for family members to share life experiences in meaningful ways. Testimonios highlighted spiritual elements within life events and often gave supernatural attribution to events. Often, testimonios were laden with interpretive work, providing commentary on why a particular outcome was meaningful or a particular lesson that was learned. The testimonios I heard from family members resembled the Pentecostal testimonies I heard at church and in this sense extended the flow of Pentecostal experience into everyday life.

Some testimonios are brief accounts, even as short as a single sentence, that remind hearers of an important event. Such accounts, when shared in my family, reminded us of how a particular event had long-lasting effects in the family's history. One of these testimonial markers was the occasional reference my father made to his aunt, Tia Hermila, as having "brought the gospel" to the rest of the family. The testimonial marker I would hear in regard to the Calvillo family conversion usually went something like this: "Mi tia Hermila trajo el evangelio a mi familia." The repetition of that and similar phrases helped me remember an important family milestone.

My mother also occasionally shared a testimonial marker about how she became Pentecostal. She referenced how her family lived in Tijuana and visited an Assemblies of God church where the Holy Spirit was at work. Her father, in a time of crisis, was invited by a congregant and took the whole family. One of my mother's schoolmates attended the church as well. This brief account situated my mother's affiliation to Borderlands Pentecostalism. On deeper inquiry, I learned that she had visited a Baptist church while living in Mexicali, Baja California; a Free Methodist church while living in San Lorenzo, Sonora; a Mexican Methodist church and an Apostolic church in Caborca, Sonora; and a Baptist church briefly in Tijuana.

The presence of the Holy Spirit at the Pentecostal church in Tijuana captivated her and her family. Yet rarely did I hear the entirety of her circuitous borderlands journey into Protestantism and then into Pentecostalism; the testimonial marker she shared focused on the key turning point that most altered her life trajectory—her affiliation with Pentecostalism.

These shorter testimonios, for some, appeared in forms of evangelism. Dropping a brief line about how one's life has been changed by God might open the door to further conversation. Such testimonios could also be offensive when shared at unsolicited moments. Nevertheless, shorter testimonios were ways to test the waters and respond according to listeners' reactions. Whether brief or extended, testimonios were key mechanisms of evangelism for most Pentecostals I knew. Some engaged in apologetic or teaching-based outreach, and scriptural propositions were common modes of evangelism, particularly when Pentecostals engaged with others who shared a sense of authority in the Bible, such as Catholics. Yet testimonios were, at the very least, in the background, undergirding the sense of assurance that Pentecostals had. Testimonios confirmed that propositional statements made were backed by a sense of personal and lived reality.

EN VICTORIA: VICTORIES OVER HARDSHIPS

Among the most prominent types of testimonios were those focused on salvation. In line with broader evangelical traditions, the greatest Pentecostal victory is to encounter God in Jesus Christ and to enter into a relationship with Jesus Christ. Pentecostal testimonios involve letting go of sin. Experiences of rupturing with one's past are common in Pentecostal narratives. Some of the most powerful testimonies I grew up hearing, for example, were testimonios of people walking away from being entrenched in a gang lifestyle, where drugs and violence dictated life opportunities. These types of testimonios were often gendered in nature, with men experiencing the most drastic changes after being lost in sin.[6]

Some church-based testimonios centered on what congregants understood as spiritual growth and spiritual victories. These were experiences in which congregants had meaningful and unique encounters with God, often bringing about significant life changes. I recall, for instance, a young woman who was given time during Sunday morning service to share about how she had experienced baptism in the Holy Spirit. She suspensefully talked about how she attended a church retreat and understood she needed something from God. During one of the worship services at the retreat, participants were invited to come forward to the altar if they wanted to receive baptism in the Holy Spirit. The woman explained that she felt compelled to go forward, not by someone around her or by the speaker but by something inside her. The deep yearning she felt for more of God was being answered by this invitation forward. She raised her hands in prayer and waited on God, and she began to speak in other tongues. Her tongue was loosed, and she was able to vocalize words that she had not spoken before. She felt a warmth move through her and an immense sense of peace. She stayed at the altar for an extended period of time and did not want to leave. The congregation affirmed her words with "amen!" and "hallelujah." In many ways, her testimonio was instructive to others about what it was like to experience the baptism in the Holy Spirit.

Testimonios were often about victories over hardship. The types of victories and hardships people shared about reflected their respective social locations. For example, during a testimonio time, an hermano shared about how he had been assaulted, but God had protected him from harm. The testimonio revealed he had lost a substantial amount of cash. This man worked in the construction industry but was undocumented and was paid in cash. The person who assaulted him likely targeted him as a laborer and intentionally intercepted him while he had cash on hand. For this hermano, it was meaningful that his body and life had been spared—this was a victory—but the testimonio was also an opportunity to share with the congregation about his economic need. His story circulated among congregants, and some helped to supplement his loss through a variety of means, whether by offering him a meal, providing funds, or recommending other jobs. Testimonios were a way to share about spiritual providence but were also a way to see providence to its end.

Testimonios could also be a way to share resources. I recall one young man who had traveled to visit family and complete important business in Mexico. Returning to the United States posed significant obstacles as he was undocumented. He took the risk of traveling to Central Mexico because the matters he needed to deal with there were urgent. In his testimonio, he shared that he was grateful to God for allowing him to go to Mexico and for bringing him back safely. He had not, as of then, made public that he was undocumented, though many church members were aware of this. He ended the testimonio by naming the place where he had crossed the border through Arizona. He told the congregation, "Esta facil por alli! Dejenme saber si quieren ir, yo les ayudo!" Essentially, he was offering his knowledge of where to cross, likely with the assistance of a coyote, to members of the congregation who had to return to Mexico. The testimonio was an informal way to share what were urgent resources for some. This does not mean that the hermano was simply there to advertise—he was grateful for his own journey. It does, however, demonstrate how the strategies employed by some immigrants were not seen as separate from God's providence and protection.

Testimonios often brought surprises. I remember a situation when one young man gave a testimony about how he had been "delivered from drugs." Many of us at church knew him while he was dealing with substance abuse issues. We saw a transformation take place in him as his pattern of drug abuse improved drastically, nearly overnight. At a special youth rally, with the church sanctuary filled to capacity, he was tasked with sharing his testimony of being delivered from drugs. He was excited to do so. As he told his story, aspects of his past life began to shine through. At one point, he described an incident of going to pick up drugs from a dealer. He referred to the drugs as "shit." The audience sat in silence. He later talked about how his dad was going to "kick his butt." Then he excused himself for saying "butt" and instead said, "Sorry, I meant I didn't want to get my ass kicked." Again, the audience seemed to hold their breath. In a Pentecostal church where curse words were a sign of being "worldly," the young man crossed some boundaries. In that moment, he was excused because his transformation had been so recent and his life change was so powerful. Through the years, the authenticity of his transformation remained.

SUPERNATURAL PENTECOSTAL REALISM

The borderlands of my parents' generation seemed a world filled with fantastical supernatural occurrences. My father especially recalls the supernaturalism in the testimonios he heard in Ciudad Juárez in the 1960s. One testimonio concerned an hermano who used to travel through the woods for work purposes and sometimes had to sleep in them. Because he had to guard himself from wild animals in the wooded terrains of Chihuahua, this man had mastered the art of sheltering in the trees of the forest overnight. On one occasion, he set himself up to rest in a tree as night set in, and he was startled by something out of a science-fiction film. According to his testimonio, he saw a flying vessel arrive on a clearing in the woods close to where he was resting. Out of this vessel, several creatures emerged, headed for the tree where he rested, and clawed at the tree trunk, attempting to reach him. The hermano prayed out loud against the beings trying to harm him. He declared, "Te reprendo en el nombre de Jesucristo!" ["I rebuke you in the name of Jesus Christ!"], a common phrase used to pray against demonic spirits. After an extended period of praying, the beings returned to their vessel and promptly departed. The hermano was able to fall asleep that night. The next morning, he came down from the tree and inspected the tree trunk, which bore marks from where he saw the creatures attempting to climb up. He said there was a remnant of a sulfur-like smell in the vicinity. This incident was understood as a demonic attack manifested as an extraterrestrial encounter. In this season, people in Mexico and the United States were fascinated by the possibilities of extraterrestrial life. Ciudad Juárez was one of the sites where people reported spotting OVNIs, the Spanish term for UFOs. In this man's testimonio, evil manifested as extraterrestrial invaders, a source of fear for a segment of the public.[7]

Another testimonio that circulated in that region involved a different man who journeyed by foot for his labor. This man talked about getting lost while journeying to a distant town that he was unfamiliar with. On his trip, a lion appeared to him and began to guide him. He began to understand the lion's instructions, which were communicated by growls. The number of growls indicated which direction that man was to travel in. The man followed the lion for miles. Eventually the lion led him close to his intended destination. In the end, the lion growled three times, which the man understood to mean "gloria a Dios [glory to God], gloria a Dios, gloria a Dios."

These testimonios were intriguing to audiences because of the supernatural elements they contained. Testimonios were a sign that God was present in people's lives and in the lives of those they knew. While these particular stories were atypical, the circulation of such testimonies infused with supernaturalism revealed an expectation among some Borderlands Pentecostals that the border between the natural and the supernatural was permeable. Such testimonial circulations revealed a type of borderlands lived theological imagination.

UNCONVENTIONAL TESTIMONIOS

Some of the testimonios that made it into my family's collection of narratives did not fit into a general formula of problem, divine encounter, and breakthrough. There is a cluster of testimonios that especially stood out to me, though they were talked about less frequently and were nearly nonexistent in the traditional church context. These alternative testimonios were ghost stories. Some stories were about ghostlike beings, but the stories themselves were ghosts—holdovers from an earlier era when a pre-Christian world or a less orthodox Christian world broke in. Still, I consider these as types of testimonios because they uncover a world of supernatural movement; they point to a world in which spiritual beings and/or spiritual powers could be harnessed to act upon the visible material world. These stories were the other side of the coin to the supernatural testimonios that were celebrated in church.

One such testimonio concerned my mother and her younger siblings and, on the surface, does not seem to deviate much from more traditional testimonios. My uncle Candelario told a story about being at the beach with my mother, Lydia, and their young siblings in the early 1960s. The family had traveled to the Gulf of Mexico for a church-related event. In their free time, the siblings headed over to the beach. My mother's siblings looked on as an ice cream vendor passed, selling *helados*. My uncle told my mother he wanted a *helado* but knew they did not have money to purchase any. My mother told him to hold on. She began to dig her hands into the sand that surrounded them. As she brought her hands up, the sand ran through her fingers, revealing several coins in her palm. She did this several times without venturing away from their resting place, gathering enough coins to buy ice cream for her siblings.

My uncle remembered this story about the coins in the sand years later in astonishment. I questioned my mother about the incident, and she said she simply got the idea to search the sand for coins and that she found enough to pay for the ice cream without going anywhere. This story, from both my mother's and uncle's perspectives, was an act of God's provision. Through this story, God demonstrated care for this group of young people, even in a most simple delight. And yet when my uncle first told me the story, he emphasized my mother's finding of the coins as if she had a certain type of gift, or what in Spanish is called a *don*. A *don* is a type of spiritual or divine giftedness that typically comes into play to help others. The word *don* is used in Latino Pentecostal circles in reference to spiritual gifts bestowed by the Holy Spirit. The term has a broader use within Mexican and borderland cultures in reference to spiritual giftedness. Whether the emphasis is placed on God's direct intervention or on spiritual giftedness activated, the testimony spoke to supernatural provision.

The potential *don* that manifested in my uncle and mother's story entered another story relayed to me by my tio Candelario. Apparently, stashes of gold were hidden in the region of Sonora, near where my ancestors lived during the campaigns of Pancho Villa, in the era of the Mexican Revolution. An uncle from my maternal grandmother's family acquired some of this gold and buried it within a plot of land that he owned. The account became legendary in the family, yet no one was able to find the gold. As a relative relayed this story to my uncle, he said, "Not just anyone can find this treasure. It's still there. It has to be someone with a special gift." My uncle responded, "I have someone who can find that treasure. That's my sister." The legend remains. The testimonio has been passed on for several generations. Again, the notion of the *don* surfaced here as a gift that was useful for provision. The redemptive possibility was that the reward would only come to a person whose heart was in the right place.

Some testimonios involved connecting with spirit beings or supernatural beings. One account circulated about a horseman in dark clothing who would appear at night at a crossroads near a family member's town and would forbid people to pass. That particular legend is part of a larger traditional story in Mexico about a mysterious horseman. Another account surfaced about a family member seeing a *duende* in the woods, a diminutive humanoid figure, in this case dressed in dark clothing. Another family member circulated a story about a living relative from a century past who was seen walking alongside an ancestor who had already passed away. These testimonios, ghost stories, helped people make sense of their surroundings. Many of these men and women lived in times of revolution or in the aftermath of revolution and were separated by borders and migrations. I wonder how many of them lost ancestors before their time or were abruptly separated from loved ones. These hauntings, I suspect, connected people to ancestors or to a spirit world of good and evil that was ever active in their lives.

After Pentecostal conversion, many of these stories were interpreted under a different light, and many were pushed below the surface of collective memory. By digging further while conversing with some of my tíos and tías, I discovered that these stories were not completely forgotten. They simmered below the surface and continued to connect people to their lineages and to a world of fantastical conflicts, gifts, and possibilities. A God that entered into these worlds had to be a God that spoke to the conditions of the people in tangible and embodied ways. Jesus Christ in the borderlands would have to be a Jesus inhabiting the unexpected, the science-fictional, the supernatural, and the ancestral. The Spirit *en la frontera* would have to be a Holy Spirit bestowing unique forms of giftedness upon people for the good of the people.

MY TESTIMONIO

For a good portion of my early life, I thought I did not have a testimonio. I was born into a Christian family, had a personal faith life, and was a good student with a promising future. My life looked nothing like the drastic pivots experienced by those who testified in my churches. I had been socialized to understand these drastic life changes as true testimonios. My salvation testimonio was simple. When I was five years of age, my mother, who would often read Bible stories to me, explained to me the story of Jesus's crucifixion. She explained further a story of redemption. Jesus had died for our sins so that we could have eternal life. And just as he had risen again, we could experience eternal life with God. I asked her how I could ask Jesus to live in my heart. I had heard this description before and thus had the language for it. As my mother pointed out, though, I myself asked her to tell me more about Jesus. I have a slight recollection of that midday conversation.

My mother used a bracelet with colored hearts intended to describe the path of Christian salvation to explain the Jesus story to me. Each color represented a distinct step in the experience of salvation. I understand that those colors have been criticized and altered in more recent years, in some cases discarded altogether. At that age, and given my particular socialization, they made sense to me. I prayed to accept Jesus into my heart. What I remember clearly about that day is that I ran out of the house with the small bracelet in hand. I ran to the grass lawn in front of our home. I tightly closed my eyelids and turned my face toward the sun. The warmth washed over me. In that moment, as the California sun grazed my shiny brown skin, I knew I would never be alone again.

Through the years, my parents would always reinforce to me that "tu tienes un testimonio." You have a testimony. As I grew older and began to serve in ministry, I came to recognize the gift of healing from generational trauma that I experienced. Life was not always easy, and I came to realize forms of systemic inequality in my communities. I also recognized that through the healing that had taken place in my family, there were burdens that I did not have to carry. Experiences I would have later in life would complicate my notions of testimonio, leaving scars and injury in my own life, but in my later teens, I came to be grateful for the life I was dealt.

Testimonios are works in progress, rehearsed and rewritten over time. Sometimes they are stories that are resolved, but most typically they are to be continued. For me, they are stories being written across generations, with a divine sense of connectedness reminding us that we are not alone.

CHAPTER THREE

Ritualized Surprises at the Altar

About twenty-five members of my youth group sat excitedly on folding chairs that Friday night, waiting for Sister Sandy, a favorite guest speaker of ours, to take to the podium. Members of my youth group at Las Buenas Nuevas Church in Norwalk agreed that she understood our struggles. Sister Sandy's giftedness was predicated on her *predicación*, her preaching, and on her *ministración*, ministry at the altar. Her preaching often brought us to solidify our commitments before God at the altar. It was through the ministry of gifted ministers like Sister Sandy that I came to see the altar as a space where sacred performances unfolded.[1]

In Borderlands Pentecostalism, altars were defined by sacred theatrics, performances of invitation, struggle, and resolution before (and with) God and others.[2] Such displays *unfolded* before audiences and *enfolded* audiences into experiencing God's presence. The line between audience and participant became blurred at the altar as all were invited to engage in outward and inward devotional labor.[3] These sequences of semipublic events were experienced as unscripted rituals, facilitating surprise, excitement, and commitment from onlookers. The most powerful expressions of sacred theatrics elicited sincere and authentic connections to God as the leading character was the Holy Spirit.

As expected, Sister Sandy's message that evening encouraged us in our Christian faith. As someone led us in worship songs, Sister Sandy prayed for us. Her voice floated over the music through the speakers, and she invited us to come forward if we desired prayer. This was the altar call. As she continued to minister through prayer, she explained that she sensed certain people were struggling with particular issues. When she named one particular issue, I remembered that some church friends of mine were dealing with this very matter. Soon, they were at the altar praying. Among the issues that she mentioned, some were negative ones that young people needed to resolve and others concerned positive opportunities. For example, some of the words Sister Sandy offered had to do with people heeding particular callings in their lives. People came to the altar to be prayed for, at first being prayed for by Sister Sandy or our youth leader, Pastor Manny; later, prayer groups formed, where young people prayed for each other.

Altars maintain a special place in Pentecostal lifeworlds[4] in part because of the ways that sacred theatrics unfold for all to see. Through the concept of theatrics, I especially highlight the sequential and spectatorial nature of altar interactions. Devotional labor related to altars may be ritualized and planned, but the performances that ensue leave space for the unexpected. In these moments at the altar, the altar becomes a space to hear from God and experience God. Sister Sandy was gifted at facilitating these moments because at the altar, her words were personal to seekers who came forward and even to some reluctant spectators. Her words were spoken publicly but were tailored to the needs of individuals. Expectations of having a personal relationship with God and experiencing God communally intersected in these altar moments. The way Sister Sandy ministered at the altar became something we anticipated. Through her ministry, and the ministry of others, young people like myself came to expect that the altar was a space where we could be surprised by God and surprised by our own responses to God.

SACRED THEATRICS

The sacred theatrics I experienced at altars shaped my expectations for surprise within Borderlands Pentecostalism. Experiences that called people into life journeys with Jesus Christ and that denoted struggling to surrender to God were especially memorable. One such scene unfolded on an occasion when I asked my father to take me to a youth service featuring several Christian Hip-Hop groups at a Victory Outreach[5] church in Anaheim, California. I was a teenager, and at the time I sought out just about any opportunity to see live Christian Hip Hop. In that season, my father and I had taken a teen from our church, called Robert,[6] under our wing; he had recently gotten out of juvenile hall. His mother appreciated when we took him around with us to church-based activities. We immediately thought of him as someone to bring with us to the concert and service.

That evening, we were treated to the funk-heavy, bass-driven beats of SSMob, echoing the West Coast sounds popular at the time. The altar became the stage for these Hip-Hop artists. The small storefront church was packed with young people, many of them wearing attire reflecting local gang culture. The lead rapper, King Shon, was a Black American who knew the ins and outs of Chicano jargon. He spoke directly to the overwhelmingly Chicano audience in a manner familiar to the community. The concert portion of the service was itself structured like many other concerts. The artists performed their songs with minimal talking but strutted across the stage, engaging the audience through call-and-response hooks. The stage quickly transformed into an altar as the artists performed the last song of their set and King Shon began to speak to the audience. It was clear he was now going to preach a message. King Shon began to share portions of his testimony. He encouraged young people to think about the particular life paths they had chosen. He shared about his life encounter with Jesus and the turning point he had experienced in that.

Since King Shon had built rapport with his audience through music, they listened to his talk. However, I observed that a group of young people toward the front of the sanctuary were less attentive to what King Shon said. Robert told me members of the Orphans, a gang from Anaheim, were present. He had grown up in Anaheim, knew the local gang culture well, and knew members of different gangs. I wondered if the group in the front was really Orphans. Then King Shon looked toward those seated in the front and said, "I heard there are some Orphans here." He then invited any of them who wanted to speak to him to come to the stage. One of the members, presumably the highest-ranking one from the group that was present, came forward. He walked onto the altar stage and faced King Shon intensely. The young man sported a common street-gang uniform: baggy jeans, a white T-shirt, a shaved head, and some "locs" (a style of sunglasses). The Orphan stood in statue-like form as if to defy King Shon. For a second, I wondered if they were going to fight, but it was obvious King Shon was not there to engage in physical struggle.

King Shon looked at the young man's dark glasses and said, "Take off your locs, mijo. Look me in the eye. You're hurting, aren't you? You don't have to hide it." King Shon challenged the young man to be his authentic self and told him that Jesus would accept him. I thought surely the Orphan would be angered by what King Shon was telling him. Instead, he removed his locs and revealed a well of tears that quickly began to flow from his eyes. He maintained his rigid countenance, but the stream of tears brightened his face. Despite his weathered face, he was probably in his late teens. Soon, King Shon embraced the young man, continued to speak to him, and began to pray for him. The energy in the room shifted. The young man prayed to give his life to Jesus Christ.

I do not know what happened to the young man who stood on the stage that night, but I do know that the altar was opened and filled up with young people wanting to give their lives to Jesus Christ. Robert was among them. He had grown up in the church, and his mother was a leader in the church, but the street life had been too tempting for him. He now wanted to turn his life around. The altar-turned-stage, turned-altar again, became a space of transformation and reconciliation to these young people who were seeking an alternative to the street life they knew. The sacred theatrics that unfolded were a turning point in the life trajectory of a young friend from my own church community.

ANSWERED PRAYERS

The sacred theatrics that unfolded at the altar often involved internal, personal striving. These are moments of internal striving that often manifest outwardly at the altar. One evening at El Buen Pastor, for example, I had felt particularly compelled to pray for a personal need. Though I was a college student living some of the most exciting moments of my life with great friends, something from my time at the altar that evening moved me to ask God for a close friend. In that altar moment, my deepest yearning that I brought to God was to have a friendship with someone who understood the many spaces I simultaneously inhabited. Though I would not have articulated it as such in that moment, I essentially sought a friendship with someone who understood the various borderlands I moved through.

One of the paradoxes of altar moments is the way that, amid the converging of noises—from music, to praying, to crying—Pentecostals often do their deepest internal listening there. In this process of listening, I would voice my inner struggles before God, articulate my yearnings in prayer, and wait for the impressions, senses, reminders, and ideas that would surface.[7] In this case, I prayed to God about how it was difficult to be known when I felt like I needed to translate aspects of myself to others. I was happy with the people I knew, but that particular season, a few friends had moved away, and I had less contact with some friends who had previously provided close camaraderie. So I kneeled at the steps of the altar and called out to God, asking that God would send a close friend in the faith to walk with me.

As I wrestled with God, not knowing if I would receive a response to my prayers, I felt a distinct inclination internally. It was as if God was telling me to open my eyes and look behind me. I had been praying with my eyes tightly shut but stood up as if to go back to my seat and opened my eyes. Instantly, as I opened my eyes, my line of sight landed on my younger brother, David. Just as quickly, an affirming thought surfaced in my mind as if it came from beyond me: "There's the person you've been praying for." I had thought this moment of resolution was bringing my altar moment to a close, but instead, the impression I received added a twist. I was hit with a wave of gratitude as I felt that God had answered my prayer, just not in the way I expected.

The catch was that my brother was only thirteen years of age. I knew that if this was the answer to my prayer, it would take some time before my brother and I would be able to have the type of relationship I was praying for. Nevertheless, that was part of the sacred drama that unfolded at the altar: to receive an answer to a prayer in a way that was unexpected. In some ways, walking away with a resolution that was outside my expectations felt even better. It was as if the answer was right before me the whole time, yet I needed to wrestle with God in order to receive the response. My brother and I were not the closest in our earlier years because we were over seven years apart. We did eventually come to have the very type of friendship that I had prayed for. To this day, he is one of my closest friends. He is a man of wisdom and someone whose opinions and insights I value significantly. That moment at the altar was something that I held on to for years and interpreted as a promise that later became reality.

PORTABLE ALTARS

The fluid nature of the locations of Pentecostal altars added to the unpredictable nature of the Pentecostal altar experience. On the one hand, there were spaces that congregations typically recognized as altars, such as stage areas that pulpits rested on in church sanctuaries. However, these were not spaces designated as permanently holy or overly restrictive in terms of the activities that took place there. Sometimes those altars were also used as spaces for less formal activities, including play or recreation. In other words, the sacralization of these spaces was tied to the practices taking place there and the moments that were identified as points of encounter with God. Pentecostals also create impromptu altars. That is, nonaltar spaces could become altar spaces under the right conditions and in the right collective moment. Moments of prayer that became increasingly unique or represented a distinct collective moment could begin to function as an altar moment even if taking place in a mundane location. For me, this was especially true within home spaces, where Pentecostal practices created moments to seek God's presence in concerted ways.

Members of the paternal side of my family often invited me to events that involved their church community, some of which were less formal events taking place at someone's home. In my late teens, I was invited to such a gathering at my aunt Martha and uncle Ismael's home. This was a youth *vigilia*, a prayer vigil, in which young people would be praying late into the night. *Vigilias* have been a staple of Pentecostal practice for generations, sometimes as part of the routine spiritual rhythm that a community engages in and sometimes focused on a particular cause or need. This particular *vigilia* had a general focus—in this case, inviting young people to pray for each other. I thought it would be a good opportunity to spend time with some of my cousins.

The *vigilia* was taking place inside an open family room at my aunt and uncle's house. When I arrived, the people there had already been praying, many of them kneeling, some walking around as they prayed. I felt as if I had walked into an altar call moment.

The *vigilia* was led by a man of prayer who had a close relationship with my extended family and was often looked to for support in matters of prayer. He was not a formal pastor, nor did he hold a formal position at a church. He was, however, seen by many in my extended family as a spiritual authority known for praying for extended periods of time, fasting, and expounding spiritual messages that would exhort others.[8] While I kneeled and prayed, I could hear him stirring, praying out loud, and speaking words of exhortation to a general audience. In many ways, his prayers announced to those within earshot which issues mattered and what we needed to pray for. Some of his prayers named specific people and particular issues they were dealing with.

Soon, a more public display of sacred performance began. The man of prayer began to invite people to be prayed for. Different young people went forward and were prayed for, sometimes sharing particular needs they had. One young man came forward, flanked by members of his family. There was something in his life that he needed to let go of, but he was struggling to do so. The man of prayer began to intercede for him. The young man broke down, cried, yelled, and was visibly struggling with something. He was not struggling with those praying for him as he had volunteered to be prayed for. I later learned he was struggling with substance abuse issues. Another young man came forward with his head down, surrounded by several friends. He whispered his prayer request to the man of prayer, who shared it with the rest of the attendees: "Este muchacho esta orando para que Dios le mande una novia" ["This young man is praying so that God will send him a girlfriend"]. Soon, several young people stood around him and began to pray for him. The young man raised his hands and prayed intently as well.

Amid the time of praying for others, a young woman burst into the room announcing that a vehicle on the street had been broken into. Another young woman, who owned the vehicle, ran out. This was interpreted as an instance of spiritual warfare. The room began to pray for the spiritual attack that had just occurred. We also prayed for the young woman whose car had been broken into as perhaps God was wanting to do something in her life and the enemy was creating a roadblock to this. The young woman left momentarily and eventually came back and was prayed for.

That prayer gathering was action-packed, lasting beyond midnight. What might have sounded to an outsider like a boring activity for young people on a Friday night was energizing to participants. The altar had been taken out of the church building and recreated within this barrio home. The space, for that moment, had been sacralized.

SPIRITUAL WARFARE

In some cases, spiritual performances at the altar involve spiritual warfare. In the Pentecostal sense, spiritual warfare is most understood as a direct confrontation with personal spiritual entities that attempt to thwart the work of God in the world and in the lives of people. Acts of spiritual warfare that ensue are intended to liberate people from spiritual oppression they may be experiencing. These forms of spiritual oppression may manifest in material and physical ways. A person experiencing oppression or in cases of more extreme demonic control, labeled as demonic possession, may lash out at those attempting to minister to them. I witnessed a variety of these types of manifestations across the spectrum of oppression and possession.

One particular instance stands out in the way it unfolded: "Give me a hug, Pastor!" With these words, the church sanctuary of El Buen Pastor became the site of a strange confrontation. "Come over here so I can give you a hug! Hahaha!" The man asking for a hug had never, to my knowledge, set foot inside the church. He entered the church sanctuary from a side exit. I was the youth minister of the church at that time, around 2003, and quickly made my way toward this man as something seemed off. As I approached him, I was able to more clearly see his appearance. He was a stocky man with tattoos on his arms. His thick mustache and speech cadence reflected the local Chicano street culture, speaking mostly English but mixing Spanish words into his speech. He was likely a *veterano*, an older gang member with influence in the barrio. "Let me give you a hug, Pastor! Hahaha," he repeated again, casting an eerie mood on the sanctuary.

I glanced over at our pastor, Pastor Victor, who stood at the altar and looked bewildered by the man's request. The man still stood by the side door of the sanctuary, several feet from the altar where the pastor stood. His laughter grew more sinister. In a matter of seconds, a cluster of men from the church surrounded him. Some women of the church stayed close to the situation, many of them praying as they stood nearby; these were intercessory prayers of spiritual warfare, praying against the spiritual attacks of the enemy potentially manifesting in the man in the sanctuary. It was as if something propelled the man forward. He showed little concern for the men around him and completely focused on the pastor. By now, it was clear he was taunting the pastor. He seemed to puff himself up, clenching his hands and flexing his arms in a menacing fashion.

What made this sudden confrontation all the stranger was an incident that had transpired moments earlier at the altar. As the Sunday morning service was ending, a young man visiting our church asked if he could share a word regarding Pastor Victor with the congregation. The visitor, Hector, knew Pastor Victor because he was a student from the Latin American Bible Institute,[9] where the pastor taught. After being allowed onto the altar's platform, with the leaders' approval, he told the church members that he sensed the pastor needed the congregation's support by praying and coming alongside him to support his vision. The congregation was moved. The pastor himself was moved and entered into a time of deep contemplation and appreciation. Some members of the church cried out, tears streamed down the faces of many, and people began to intercede for the pastor. A circle of leaders and congregants had gathered around Pastor Victor and prayed for him at the altar. The man who came in off the street looking for Pastor Victor walked through the sanctuary door just as prayer for the pastor was dissipating.

As a group of men restrained the menacing man, his words escalated, and he was now hurling curse words at the pastor. Someone from the church called the police. Soon, officers appeared at the church doors and subdued the man, but he continued to utter words against the pastor. Congregants continued to pray. I followed the scene as closely as I could and heard the man repeat a Bible verse multiple times: "At the name of Jesus every knee should bow, of things in heaven, and things in earth, and things under the earth; and that every tongue should confess that Jesus Christ is Lord."[10] Even as he was being handcuffed, I heard the man continue to repeat the verse. As he was taken away, congregants convened, and the scene slowly de-escalated.

When the incident had originally taken place, most church members I spoke with understood it as a spiritual attack on the pastor, an incident of spiritual warfare with an outward, physical manifestation. The man could have been under the influence of drugs, given the actions and attitudes he exhibited, but I, too, could not help but think of this incident as a manifestation of evil. I suspected these dimensions—substance abuse and demonic activity—were not mutually exclusive in this situation. The confrontation, for many, confirmed notions of how spiritual warfare was not an abstract occurrence in Borderlands Pentecostalism. Such incidents had real material and physical consequences. While our battle was not against flesh and blood, it was on flesh and blood that warfare was most acutely experienced.

This man had likely already faced a disproportionate amount of systemic evil, despite his role in this incident of spiritual warfare. He had simultaneously made choices that brought him to enact evil and had lent his body to a work of anger and harm. In this way, he exercised agency, even as he allowed himself to be swept up by something beyond himself. Nevertheless, he was not an evil incarnate. His tattoos delineating his gang activity pointed to a life of hardship and that he was someone who found solace in the camaraderie of the neighborhood gang. His language, cadence, and inflection indicated he had been iteratively shaped by the culture of the street. His interactions with police further indicated that he was a *veterano* with experiences of being surveilled and adjudicated on. Systemic warfare had been inflicted on this man, and his lashing out marked him as a victim of this war, both spiritual and sociological.

Displays of spiritual warfare at the altar were understood as individual confrontations with evil spiritual entities manifested in individuals' lives, yet these encounters were much more than that. Often, these were manifestations of structural harm meted on individuals, especially members of vulnerable and marginalized communities. This also meant that in the name of spiritual warfare, further harm could be inflicted on these vulnerable populations. Nevertheless, in positive encounters I witnessed, people consented to being ministered to. Often, these incidents unfolded at the altar or in connection to altar calls. The altar became a site of liberation, healing, and restoration in such cases.

POSSIBILITIES

The sacred theatrics of the altar in Borderlands Pentecostalism significantly shaped the identities of community members. The interactive, boundary-blurring sequences that unfolded in public sight were memorable precisely because of the ways they were personal and communal all at once. The dimensions of struggle at the altar called for full attention and deep commitment. At the altar, the faithful struggled internally and externally, they accompanied others in their struggles, and they were sometimes confronted with agents of spiritual opposition. Many personal connections developed through these sacred theatrics as people encountered kindred souls.

Altars were not a panacea. Sometimes they were sites of disappointment. Sometimes they were sites of manipulation and abuse. Yet the moments that most stood out to me were those in which people expressed sincere concern, vulnerability, and solidarity at the altar. Typically, when I observed long-term positive effects in someone who was ministered to at the altar, it was because there was a long-term support system in place and a rhythm of spiritual practices that empowered the person to continue on in self-reflection and holistic spiritual growth. The unpredictability of the altar and the possibilities for divine encounters energized seekers to continue looking toward the altar as a site of ritualized surprise.

PART TWO

Rites of Passage

CHAPTER FOUR

Border Baptism

"Strength's in the pack!" my football team and I barked out at the top of our lungs. Football practice was about to finish, and the coach was teaching our team a new chant. We each thrust a hand into the center of a circle and broke from practice as the coach called out, "Coyotes on three, coyotes on three."

"Coyotes!" we all yelled, breaking away from the circle.

Throughout the chants, motivational speeches, and drills, the language of kinship came through loud and clear. In these last days of summer before the coming season, our coaches told us we were training to be brothers, to be a family. Soon, we would face an initiation rite that was meant to not only prepare us individually for the season but also bring us together: hell week. Hell week marked the start of the high school football season. This week stretched athletes to their physical and mental limits two weeks before their first football game; coaches gave us the impression that if we could endure hell week together, we would succeed during the regular season. My junior year of high school would be my first season playing at the varsity level and my first season playing under the stadium lights. I knew if I could get through this ritual, this baptism of sorts, I would be a respected member of the squad.

My understandings of community membership largely came from my church experience. I was familiar with membership rites. In my Latino Pentecostal church, for example, we emphasized two baptisms: baptism in water and baptism in the Spirit. Both baptisms encompassed a deep sense of belonging. These sacramental experiences enlivened a type of spiritual kinship for me. They pointed to a deep commitment and communion with Jesus Christ and also to a sense of belonging within a community of people orienting their lives toward Jesus Christ. These were heightened moments of kinship when my ties to the community showed bright, as they were recognized not only by self but also by the community itself. These experiences pointed me toward a sense of kindom,[1] furthered by Ada Maria Isasi-Diaz as a familial conception of spiritual ties predicated on a reciprocal, mutual mode of belonging and challenging sexist, hierarchical modes of belonging and participation.

I dreaded the upcoming experience of hell week as a gateway to achieving this deep sense of kinship that the coaches promised. With this initiation came new responsibilities and new expectations. As with church baptisms, I perceived I would now be under scrutiny as a public representative of the community. I wondered if I would fail my communities.

I had some time to prepare for this grueling initiation. Team members were given two weeks off from summer practice before hell week commenced. Coaches expected athletes to train on their own so as to be ready for the week. That summer in 1994, I had doubts about my ability to prepare for the coming football season given my family's schedule. Our usual summer trip consisted of traveling to see my grandfather in San Luis, Arizona, during the weeks off from football practice. My grandfather lived in a mobile home walking distance from the US-Mexico border. The earliest memories I have of visiting my tata Candelario are of him living on the Mexican side of the border in San Luis Río Colorado, Sonora. By the early 1980s, he had relocated to the US side of the border, not far from where he previously lived. As a *fronterizo*, someone of the borderlands, he conducted business on both sides of the border and maintained ties with acquaintances across the port of entry. I would be spending my training time in these borderlands.

A DIFFERENT RITE

With hell week on my mind, little did I know I would encounter a different type of initiation rite in the coming days. This initiation uncovered the long and complicated relationship I had with borders, particularly at ports of entry. In my childhood, crossing the border elicited fear. I grew up hearing about family members who could not cross the border freely and people who were detained at the border. Even as a US-born person, I was warned to respond properly to immigration agents at the border to avoid being detained. Yet the borderlands were also places of much joy. The geographic borderlands represented family to me. My father grew up in Ciudad Juárez, which bordered El Paso, Texas. My mother spent early years in San Luis Río Colorado, Sonora, bordering its sister city of San Luis, Arizona; she also lived for a time in Tijuana, bordering San Diego, California. Both were *fronterizos*, people of *la frontera* who were used to crossing borders. To visit the borderlands brought me a sense of familiarity. Borders, to me, represented the elements of my home culture on display for all to see, except that rather than experiencing the culture alongside spectators and scrutinizers, creators and adapters of the culture curated this space. *La frontera* felt like home in many ways.

The spirituality I knew was also very much a *frontera* spirituality. When we visited these regions, we often attended church with family on the Mexico side of the border. Weddings often took place at churches in Mexico, even if that meant a substantial number of people crossed the border to attend. I loved how Sunday morning church meant getting up and going to Mexico to worship in community there. When we traveled deeper into Mexico, we would also visit churches. It was a natural extension of my family's *fronterizo* culture. I have memories of sitting with children of my age in Sunday school classes in Mexico while traveling.

My ability to move across borders was a privilege, and I recognized it as such since my childhood. We had family members who could not go into Mexico because if they did, they could not return to the United States. Others would have liked to come to the United States to visit but were limited in their ability to do so. My family, on the other hand, had gained the status and documents that allowed us to move back and forth. Nevertheless, something haunted me. I grappled with the fear of crossing the border in my early childhood. I wondered what would happen if the border agents who inspected us when we arrived at the US port of entry did not believe I belonged to my parents or that I was a US citizen. At the time, border agents looked through the window of vehicles at inspection points and acknowledged all passengers. Passengers were expected to share their documents and/or declare, "American citizen." I practiced this phrase often: "American citizen!" I made sure I left no doubt that my English was as near perfect as could be. If we traveled with cousins, they would often prepare me: "Are you ready?"

I had internalized the stories of border enforcement that people in my communities, including family members, had experienced. While border enforcement was not what it is today, I grew up hearing stories of evasion and maneuvering in order to make a life in the United States. For example, one relative evaded border patrol agents in the 1970s by joining a group of young men playing baseball at a park near a port of entry in Arizona. He took off his shirt and pushed himself into the baseball lineup as border patrol agents searched the area for him.

Another family account circulated about a relative tasked with picking up another relative who was about to cross the border into the United States in the 1970s. One relative in San Diego made a call from a payphone to the other in Tijuana and commenced to chart out their connection point. Soon after the start of the conversation, static and other voices began to interfere with their call. The relative in the United States grew nervous, thinking their call was being intercepted. He used an impromptu coded phrase to encourage the relative in Mexico to make a move: "Joven, dejese venir sin mencionar nombres" ["Young man, come on over without mentioning any names"]. Eventually, the relative from Mexico arrived at the appointed destination point, and all were safe. The phrase stayed within my family's lexicon and became an inside joke. Sometimes, when a family member wanted to goad another into action or tease them without giving away too many details, they would say, "Joven, dejese venir sin mencionar nombres." This subdued humor was a way to cope with border realities. The border was present even when it was not. The deeper reality that our families and communities still dealt with issues of citizenship and legality, even if some of us were US-born or documented, was present, and I internalized it.

SEEING THE LIGHT

That summer in San Luis, I wrestled with what to do about training. The local temperatures surpassed 120°F. Locals like my tata Candelario survived by maxing out their window cooler units. These mechanisms exerted maximum energies during the heat; I wondered how I would exert my energies. When we visited my grandfather, we typically stayed with the Garcia family, family friends since decades ago who were essentially kin to us. The Garcia family lived next to extensive agriculture fields. Irrigation canals ran alongside their neighborhood, extending outward and outlining the crops in the area. Typically, these canals were lined by dirt roads traversed by work trucks dedicated to agriculture labor.

The roads that ran alongside the canals offered opportunities for training, if the time was right. Once the sun went down, the heat was bearable. I decided to go running at night. Right before stepping out, I told my parents I would be running on the service roads alongside the fields. As I walked out the backdoor of the Garcia home, I thought I heard my father say, "Por alla te veo" ["I'll see you out there"]. Once my feet hit the dirt road, my focus was on getting my heart rate up to prepare for the sprint workouts that the coaches would unleash on us. I plodded along, feeling the small jagged rocks under my sneakers. The moon lit my way and shimmered over the dark, shallow waters of the parallel canal.

When I picked up the pace, I allowed my imagination to take over as I thought about what it would feel like to finally play under the lights. I was a lineman, blocking for playmakers on offense and defending against running backs on defense. Crowds rarely noticed linemen unless we failed to do our job. What if I drew attention to myself by making an error? The lights would reveal it all!

I moved deeper into my imagination as I ran along. The path grew less and less familiar as I ran farther from the Garcia family home and left behind the areas we had explored as children. On the other side of the canal, I could see that the terrain was sandier and more rugged. The outline of low shrubs and loose dirt clods presented an opportunity. Perhaps my legs would experience more resistance on that side of the canal. I found a point at which a bridge crossed the canal into the uneven terrain.

I jogged across and looked to the stream of water below. The waters in the canals came from the Colorado River. The shadowy canals gave the illusion of fog. A few miles away were the Reservation lands of the Cocopah people, variantly known as "the river people" or "cloud people," the latter a reference to the fog that would emerge in some parts of the Colorado River. The Cocopah people who stewarded these lands for generations had been documented by Spanish explorers, such as Juan de Oñate y Salazar,[2] since the seventeenth century and perhaps earlier. I was trudging on their land. Their community had been traversed by the border, and now I was crossing their sacred waters.

Running the more rugged terrain did make the run more difficult. Soon, I began to slip back into my imagined scenarios under the stadium lights. As I ran past the shadowy shrubs, I imagined them as players on an opposing team. I pictured myself in a different role, as a running back, running with the football in hand, approaching defenders and picking up speed. I would slow down for intervals and jog along. I wanted to get the technique right. I mimicked some of the great running backs who had played for our high school recently. I zigzagged to avoid one of the defenders. I could escape them, but there was no escaping the lights. The lights would make everything visible.

The lights were in my imagination. But suddenly they were not. I came to an immediate halt. The light was real. I was immersed in the light, baptized by it. Everything beyond the light was imperceptible. I froze. From beyond the light, a voice spoke. Not the voice of the stadium announcer in my imagination nor the hoarse voice of my coach but certainly a commanding voice that demanded my attention. "Identifíquese!" ["Identify yourself!"] said a woman. I squinted and could see the silhouette of two people. Behind them, I could make out the shape of a truck. These people had materialized right before my eyes. As they stepped forward, I had little question about who they were: border patrol agents. Unknowingly, I had crossed into heavily surveilled land. I remained frozen, gripped by fear. Dumbfounded, I struggled to respond. Did they want my name? Did they want to know what I was doing? I floundered around for what I should tell them. By then I could see their uniforms as they stepped closer to me. I had no identification with me. I had run out of the house with my pockets completely empty. I wondered if the border patrol agents would take me in. The light exposed my fear.

Then another voice broke into the scene: "Él es mi hijo. Es que salió a entrenar porque está en un equipo de deporte en su escuela" ["This is my son. He went out to train because he is on a sports team at his school"]. My father had followed me as he had told me. I never saw him until then, but somehow he had followed my trail all the way into the more rugged terrain. He had caught up to me just as the border patrol had apprehended me. I vaguely recall that my father exchanged words with them; that was enough for the border patrol agents to let me go.

I was in a half-dream state as the two of us walked back to the Garcia family home. Soon after, the memory became hidden deep in my psyche. It was temporarily forgotten. Yet, while the images of that night were stored away from my retrievable memories, my gratitude for my father remained, manifesting in diffuse ways.

APPREHENDED MEMORIES

The memory of my encounter with the border patrol agents did not surface for nearly twenty-five years. The political discourse of 2018 was ablaze with debate over the policy of apprehending minors at the border. As the images of children being held in cages flooded media outlets, my encounter with the border patrol agents returned to my conscious memory. My experience at the border had not been like that of these children and teens being held for extended periods of time in dehumanizing conditions while undergoing humiliating bureaucratic processes. My experience was short-lived and was quickly resolved. Still, the fear I felt in that instance, the powerlessness, the inability to think clearly, came back to me. I thought about how much more difficult the experience must have been for the children being apprehended presently.

In exploring my family's history, I came to uncover my family's complicated multigenerational relationship to the US-Mexico border. My maternal grandmother Josefina Fraijo's ancestors long ago had lived in what would become the borderlands in the region of modern Arizona, not far from Tucson, since before the United States annexed the territory. Some of these ancestors were settlers, and others were Indigenous Americans. The Fraijo family resided on land through the Santa Cruz land grant. When the United States annexed the territory, arrivals from eastern US states disputed portions of this land. Eventually, the Fraijo family and other residents lost rights to portions of it. The extended Fraijo family splintered into various branches, some settling in the United States and others in Sonora, Mexico. The former became US citizens, and the latter remained Mexican citizens; my line was the latter. When I first heard the saying "we didn't cross the border; the border crossed us," I thought the phrase was corny. Years later, I realized that the border had actually divided my ancestors.

BAPTIZED INTO KINSHIP

My ties to my father, a man who had only recently completed a drawn out and complicated process to gain residency, helped me avoid further scrutiny and possible detention by the border patrol. This kinship bond was made evident in that moment and resolved my situation. In the borderlands, the bonds of kinship, chosen and given, are a powerful force. My father's words "El es mi hijo," which broke into the initial interrogation of the border patrol agents, are reminiscent of a declaration made in a scene from Matthew's Gospel.[3] "Este es mi hijo" ["This is my son"] are the words that laid a foundation in the gospel narrative for the start of Jesus's ministry. These are the words that broke into the scene when Jesus was baptized by John the Baptist. It is a heavenly declaration of divine kinship between Father and Son, Parent and Child. Jesus's ministry started with a divine declaration of kinship. More than declaration of kinship made to the present public, it was an affirmation of kinship made to Jesus himself. When one's authorization comes into question, kinship provides affirmation. This kinship is a relational reality, not a biological one.

Jesus's baptism took place in a borderlands space, at the Jordan River. John the Baptist, a figure who stood between eras in the biblical narrative, spent much of his time in the wilderness, and the Jordan River was on the edge of this wilderness space. In conducting his baptisms at the Jordan River, John the Baptist employed a space that signified crossing into and demarcating change. As Rachel Havrelock notes, "Many lines of continuity intersect in the borderlands East of the Jordan."[4] These lines are layered into the Hebrew Scriptures as stories of encounter, transformation, and change of direction in the Jordan River Valley. Jesus crossed into this space for the start of his public ministry and maintained an ongoing relationship to borderland spaces.

The kinship that was declared in the account of Jesus's baptism was coupled with an additional sign of empowerment: the descent of the Holy Spirit upon Jesus. In the account of Jesus, kinship was coupled with anointing and empowerment. The Holy Spirit, as an active, animating, life-giving divine figure, descended on Jesus as Jesus's divine kinship was declared. This connection between Jesus and the Holy Spirit was displayed in the borderlands. Kinship and anointing, kinship and empowerment, kinship and calling are intertwined. The call to life, the call to traverse boundaries that cause death,[5] was tied up with kinship. So often it is kinship, chosen and given, that calls immigrants to traverse borderlands. I return to Ada Maria Isasi-Diaz's[6] notion of kindom in distinction to an imperialistic notion of kingdom. Where a kingdom conquers, a kindom unites.

My baptism at the borderlands took place through crossing waters, immersion in light, and amid conflicting voices, one that questioned my status in the land and another that affirmed my kinship. This baptism took place after I crossed the irrigation waters that drew their flow from the Colorado River and were long cared for by the Cocopah people, whose lands remain divided by the border. It took place in lands that my ancestors had traversed for generations. While the memory remained hidden, my embodied movement through the borderlands was changed.

My father did not appeal to my citizenship when he negotiated with the border patrol agents. If he did, I surely do not remember it. I remember that he appealed to our kinship. Kinship is reflected in the divine relationship between parent and child displayed in the Gospels. In the borderlands, the Spirit brings this to light. The ways that borders stretch kinship to its ontological limits present an opportunity to envision how images of divine kinship challenge current sociopolitical realities. The Spirit in the borderlands presents opportunities to affirm the humanity of people torn from the very kinship webs that make them who they are and affirm the core of their existence. The Spirit invites people to acknowledge how actual ecologies,[7] which entail forms of kinship as well, are being torn asunder by structures of division. Likewise, the Spirit at the borderlands invites people to uplift the voices of Indigenous communities who have stewarded these lands for eons and to place increased control in their hands. The Spirit *en la frontera* guides us to envision new futures on the edges of empire and toward a future beyond empire.

A LIMINAL CLARITY

In the summer of 2023, I returned to the familiar borderlands of Yuma, Arizona, not far from the site where I was stopped by the border patrol as a teen. I made arrangements to visit the border again with another family member. Early one midweek morning, my cousin

Aimee drove us alongside the border wall to visit a reception site for asylum seekers. Aimee volunteered with AZ-CA Humanitarian Coalition, an organization offering hospitality and aid to migrants arriving at the border. At the site, volunteers provided water, food, bathroom access, and other supplies for recent arrivals aiming to open asylum cases in the United States after turning themselves in to border authorities. On arriving, I took in the diverse backgrounds of migrants present. Several wore Muslim kufis; some spoke French; some were African, Middle Eastern, Central American, and East Asian. The soil under my feet was familiar, but I could not ignore how the border terrain continued to shift under the machinations of people in power in disparate locales.

Aimee narrated to me how site interactions typically went, sharing about recent tragedies that had occurred there, as well as some meaningful connections she had made with migrants. As migrants were transported away, Aimee told of how migrants sometimes gifted her items[8] from their homelands. These were items migrants chose to leave behind, lessening their loads, sometimes due to insecurity they felt about reclaiming them once in custody. These proceedings were disempowering, yet migrants' humanity broke through in these acts of giving—of giving back—a passing gesture of trust, an exercising of agency, a fleeting kinship in the borderlands. Some insisted, "Please, please take it!" as they handed items to her. Remaining items were typically thrown away or recycled. She showed me a coin purse that someone had recently left behind from Turkey.

As we walked back to Aimee's car, a group of three migrants crossed the waters of the river on a small bridge near the border wall. They approached us inquiring about the reception site, and we pointed it out to them. As they began to walk away, one young man stepped back toward us. Sporting a broad smile, he extended his fist in my direction, signaling with a nod that he wanted us to bump fists. As our fists met,[9] his smile beamed further, and he walked away briskly, catching up to his friends. I felt a spark in the young man's spirit. I prayed that the Spirit *en la frontera* would take him to where he needed to go. I drove off with my kin, observing the back roads that cut through the agricultural fields. From dirt mounds alongside the irrigation canals, the eyes of the border in the form of burrowing owls looked back at me. "You'll be back" one seemed to nod.

As for my junior season of football, I ended up quitting after hell week. The week was one of the toughest physical experiences I ever endured, and I proved that I belonged. But I decided to focus on academics that year. I aimed to graduate at the top of my class and realized that football would put a strain on my most rigorous academic year. I rejoined my team the following year and played my senior season. Though I never spoke about my border baptism those years, in retrospect I wonder if something within me shifted. My body held on to that which quickly slipped away from my conscious memory. I proved that I could succeed at hell week. I crossed a threshold. Yet who I needed to be, for myself and for my community, became clearer after that week. My border baptism brought a liminal clarity.

CHAPTER FIVE

Spirit Empowerment

The silhouette of pine trees blended into a jagged skyline cutting into the bright starlit night. My nine-year-old eyes wandered back and forth between the expansive firmament, the campfire flames, and the preacher who invited the audience of several hundred boys to listen. I had attended many camps with the Royal Rangers, a Boy Scout-like ministry associated with my church denomination, where we would learn outdoor skills, play sports, compete in Bible-knowledge contests, and attend evening services. I knew what the focus would be for this night service; as expected, the preacher, a man called Two-Belts, said he would be talking about how the baptism in the Holy Spirit gave power to God's people. His sermon was based on the biblical story of Samson and how the Holy Spirit would come upon him, giving him extrahuman strength. The preacher integrated the book of Acts and how the early disciples of Jesus were empowered through baptism in the Holy Spirit. The charge to the young listeners was that we had been called to share the good news of Jesus Christ.

To many young Borderlands Pentecostals, the promise that the Holy Spirit would empower us to overcome barriers and exercise unique spiritual gifts was hope-filled and energizing. Yet experiences of seeking Holy Spirit empowerment were not merely about feeling powerful. Moments of Spirit empowerment, both through baptism in the Holy Spirit and gifts of the Spirit, paradoxically allowed us to experience a vulnerability[1] that challenged the power hierarchies we encountered in the world around us.[2] Even though these experiences could create alternative hierarchies,[3] they were felt as moments when we let down our guard before God. The empowerment we felt in those instances was not about being better or greater than others but about being authentically known. That is, empowerment seemed to come while being the truest self before God. As we emerged from these moments, some of us moved through the world with a sense of confidence and purpose, having been met by our Creator. These moments of seeking Spirit empowerment carried a promise of being able to move through the world authentically, even if the public—or the church—did not understand us. For those living on the edges of society and constantly monitoring one's sense of self, the promise of being empowered as an authentic self was worth striving for.

ANTICIPATION FOR THE HOLY SPIRIT

The message that night at camp was one I expected. I had heard about the baptism in the Holy Spirit for years now, even as a nine-year-old. I had seen people receive the baptism in the Holy Spirit at church services, crowded revivals, and intimate prayer gatherings. When the Spirit came upon someone, they were overwhelmed with God's palpable presence. Many cried or called out to God. Some shook and fell to the floor, with friends or church volunteers present to catch them and ensure their safety. This was not just any moment of experiencing God's presence. Baptism in the Holy Spirit was a milestone in the life of a believer. The power that believers received was not only of personal benefit but also furthered the work of the church in the world. As I understood, a church where people experienced baptism in the Holy Spirit was a church that had a vibrant relationship to the Holy Spirit.

The outward sign of receiving the baptism in the Holy Spirit, we were taught, was speaking in tongues.[4] Pastors told us that baptism in the Holy Spirit should normally be accompanied by other benefits such as personal holiness and increased awareness of God's presence. Still, speaking in tongues captured my imagination. It was something that observers could point to. Church leaders could count the number of people who had been baptized in the Holy Spirit based on how many people spoke in tongues. So at camps like the Royal Ranger "Pow Wow," there was hope that some campers would receive the baptism in the Holy Spirit as evidenced by speaking in tongues, and this could be celebrated in community. The preacher that night explained how, when the Holy Spirit came upon the early disciples, they spoke in tongues. We were encouraged to consider how God gave this utterance, and we did not need to fake or imitate it. We simply needed to let go,[5] and at the right time, God would give us the baptism in the Holy Spirit. Through our seeking and surrendering, the Spirit would come upon us, and we would speak in tongues.

As a committed Pentecostal boy, I wanted to be a witness to the gospel[6]; however, I was often shy. I needed this baptism. I wanted the Holy Spirit to empower me to share the love of Jesus with others and make a difference in others. I had a tremendous motivation to go up to the altar that night at the Royal Ranger camp. When the preacher invited campers forward to seek the baptism in the Holy Spirit, I went. Preachers could not *promise* that at a given moment people would experience the Holy Spirit baptism, but they often emphasized that the baptism was *promised* to all believers. I believed that the promise was for me and that the promise was for that night. During camp altar calls, boys would come forward with varying degrees of confidence. I went forward confidently. Clusters formed throughout the floor space. Adult leaders joined their respective groups and began to pray with campers. I closed my eyes and began to pray for the baptism.

Even at that age, my understanding of the Holy Spirit was deeply rooted. I wanted the close connection to God and the power and authority to serve God that came with the baptism.[7] I also wanted to place myself in God's hands as I would need to do in waiting for the baptism. What began as a quiet prayer shifted into an audible calling out from me and others: "Jesus!" Some of us began to stretch out our arms, lifting our hands up and reaching out to embrace God. The leaders would often place a hand on our shoulders or upper backs and pray alongside us. At moments, I paused from my prayers and scanned the skies above, thinking of the expansive universe, how God was present throughout, and how great it was that God could be known by us. As I thought of God's greatness, I would begin to call out again.

It is difficult to know how long we prayed for, but we certainly pressed on. We waited for the Spirit to show up in a palpable way. Some began experiencing the Spirit, and some spoke in tongues. "Just praise Jesus," some leaders would encourage us periodically if they saw we were intent on receiving the baptism. By then, I was completely overwhelmed by a sense of God's embrace. The more I released myself in the moment, the more I felt I was enveloped in God's presence. It was as if I were floating in a stream of water. In the sensation of extended peace, I allowed my verbal capacities to relax. I focused on the goodness of God. I focused on how much I wanted to know God. I became less focused on achieving something and more focused on God's presence.

Then it happened. I uttered a string of syllables. At first, I repeated the same syllables several times. Then other syllables began to flow out, not many but enough to where I felt they meant something. Others gathered around me and prayed with me. Tears streamed down my face. I felt an overwhelming sense of love. I felt love from friends and leaders, and I felt love within me, coming from the inside and moving out. Was I the one speaking, or was God speaking through me? I felt I had some control and also that I had given my control over to God. I continued to pray in tongues. Hands raised, I thanked God for this beautiful moment.[8] I did not want the moment to end. I felt vulnerable and braver than ever. I felt as if God had infused me with courage. I knew God was close.[9] I had crossed into a spiritual borderland. I was in a liminal space,[10] a space that was physical and material but also otherworldly. Connected to the expanse beyond me, I was in my body, was my body, and was more than my body all at once. I breathed deeply and took it all in.

COMMUNAL SPIRIT BAPTISM

The vulnerability and empowerment that young Borderlands Pentecostals experienced through Holy Spirit baptism relate to the simultaneously deeply personal and deeply collective nature of these moments. Like a personal testimonio of salvation, receiving the baptism could not be claimed by proximity to others who had experienced it or through familial or social transference. Everyone who experienced the baptism had a testimonio of their own. It was a "between God and me" moment. And yet, so often, these were public experiences. Occasionally, someone reported receiving the baptism in private, but typically these experiences happened in front of others at the altar, during a prayer gathering, and/or due to a public invitation from a preacher. The experience facilitated a sense of belonging. The communal aspect of the baptism was intertwined with the broader communal camp experience. Our times together throughout the camp attuned us toward seeking the Spirit together. Though I did not have the awareness then, the camp activities influenced my understandings of spiritual striving in community.

The interactions with leaders and peers—the laughter, competitions, and friendships—were part of the spiritual yearning and striving that developed within me and culminated in the baptism. The Royal Ranger group I belonged to benefited from the commitment of volunteer leaders, who helped set the stage for our spiritual striving, even if they themselves were not particularly spiritual. My father, who was a leader in the program, helped to recruit many of these volunteers. He had regular volunteers who were present week in and week out, and he recruited additional volunteers to attend camps and help supervise campers. As a youngster, I often found myself in conversation with these leaders, listening to their stories, gleaning from their wisdom. These were always working-class men, either immigrants from Latin America or Los Angeles–area Chicanos. Often, they shared stories about their own upbringings and unique lessons they learned.

I was especially interested in these men's stories of Latin America. I recall being intrigued as one man shared about serving in the

Guatemalan military. He spoke of how he and his comrades were trained to trek for miles on end and ate meals rapidly before resuming their journeys. A Honduran man revealed his knife skills by whittling an intricately designed staff out of a tree branch that he picked up around camp. Another man, the father of a friend, played in a Mexican regional *grupo* and composed a song for our camp group as part of a competition. Other groups marveled at his talent. He was not able to use these talents at church, though, because he rarely attended church and played for a non-Christian band. He was a rare volunteer allowed to participate as a nonchurch member because his son was a church regular.

My uncle Pete Hernandez was a regional Royal Ranger leader involved in an affiliated group called the Frontiers Camping Fraternity (FCF). FCF allowed members to expand their outdoor survival skills and learn about the lifestyle of North American frontier explorers from past centuries. The group was built around the practices and lore of early North American settlers. Along with emulating European-descent explorers, some FCF members dressed as Indigenous Americans. FCF members were camp leaders who put on skits and taught object lessons to young campers during evening services. Potential members went through a strenuous process to join the fraternity and, once admitted, were seen as models to be emulated by the young participants.

There was something different about my uncle Pete as an FCF leader. When FCF leaders appeared during night services, Uncle Pete wore Apache regalia. He was known as White Eagle. My uncle was not putting on an act as he was actually Apache. His ancestors were originally from Arizona, and his family migrated to San Diego County, where he grew up. I knew his regalia and the stories he told during our camp meetings were real. He was sharing a true part of himself with us campers. There was a sense of pride that welled up in me as I saw my uncle leading at these camps. He was respected—feared, even. To me, it meant something that he stood there as an Indigenous American man and called out to many of us brown kids, disconnected from our Indigenous ancestries, for a deeper, more authentic relationship with God.[11]

The camp experience, I learned, was an opportunity to draw from a different self, one that was outside the ordinary, mundane world. These men were often rugged and spoke gruffly. But they also had moments of tenderness and joy. Particularly when they would let their guards down and become engulfed in creating or storytelling. Camp was formative for the boys and hard work for the volunteers, but it was also clear that these working-class, mostly immigrant men were able to tap into a space of spiritual seeking. It was an opportunity to activate gifts and lean into creative inclinations that seldom came out in their primary livelihoods. Within this larger context of empowerment, these volunteers shared aspects of their life stories that they normally could not share at church or back home. It was as if empowerment, vulnerability, and creativity went together. I gleaned then that when people gave themselves to serving God, hidden skills and gifts were revealed. Camp was a place to experience these surprises. While baptism in the Holy Spirit was described to us as a standardized experience, for me it emerged from a Latin American context of creativity.

Opportunities to testify about baptism in the Holy Spirit blended vulnerability with celebration. Returning home, we shared about the blessings we had received at camp and were embraced by our diverse congregation because of this unifying experience. I volunteered to share about having received the baptism in the Holy Spirit at our evening testimony service back home. It was a moment of celebration as different boys spoke of their encounters with God at camp. There was vulnerability in sharing about deeply emotional experiences. Boys searched for words to describe their experiences; some boys choked up, either with nervousness or as tears welled up when they spoke. The congregation applauded. Parents hugged their children. When campers did not have parents or guardians present, adults from the congregation drew near to encourage and congratulate them. Campers felt a sense of pride as we shared the moment together. Even as the initial celebration of Spirit baptism soon faded into the broader repertoire of Pentecostal practices and opportunities, those moments of celebration mattered. In these moments, testifiers were affirmed in their spiritual striving and their spiritual commitment to the broader community. Those who had received the Spirit baptism were supposed to want more of God and inspire others to experience more of God. The moments of celebration were something I looked forward to and simultaneously understood as momentous.

WORDS OF THE SPIRIT

Though I grew up in congregations that purported to embody gender equality when it came to ministering in the fullness of the Holy Spirit, gendered boundaries still structured Holy Spirit encounters. As a child and a teen, I often observed that baptism in the Holy Spirit was mediated by men in positions of leadership. At the same time, women in my church communities often engaged in ministering through the gifts of the Spirit within the broader community.[12] These were moments when women exercised spiritual gifts under the power of the Holy Spirit, such as speaking in tongues regularly, prophecy, and words of wisdom. Spirit baptism was a doorway into an experience with other spiritual gifts, and in my communities, it was often women who exercised these gifts and prayed for others to receive them. Moreover, men, more so than women, tended to initiate the invitation to receive the baptism in the Holy Spirit before mixed-gender audiences, but women had more parity in exercising the gifts of the Holy Spirit publicly.

The gifts of the Spirit often operated during altar call moments at which congregants were invited to come forward and seek deeper encounters with God. In these moments, I might have heard especially women speaking in tongues, ministering to each other in prayer, and offering words of wisdom to those they ministered to. Words of wisdom, in this case, were words of spiritual insight directed at a specific person, often offering some type of directive, a word of uplift, or even a word challenging individuals in areas of their lives. Even in cases where women engaged in these ministry moments in a gendered fashion—that is, primarily among women—the proximity among congregants at the altar provided the opportunity for men to experience the ministry of women. These moments of *ministración*, or altar ministry, in my contexts involved close proximity across genders, unlike stricter Pentecostal communities where cross-gender ministry is highly monitored and/or restricted. The altar, then, provided a space where women's ministries in the spiritual gifts flowed with freedom.

Even as some women were limited in terms of institutional leadership, many ministered across gendered lines by exercising their spiritual gifts publicly. Women who were in positions of leadership, especially evangelists and pastors, were the most likely to publicly minister through the gifts of the Spirit in the churches I attended. That is, women who had formally recognized ministries and positions had more authority to minister to both men and women. One of my youth pastors, Mary Arias, for example, excelled at mentoring young men and women in their gifts. It was important and formative for the teens of the church to have experienced her ministry and that she was given a formal platform to do so.

I also recall the ministry of a woman evangelist, Dina Santamaria, who would speak powerfully about her evangelistic trips to various nations. Her sermons would often include vivid testimonies of miracles and of God's healing and saving acts. I especially remember being captivated by her stories of spiritual warfare, where she described in detail experiences of being confronted by demonic spirits when ministering liberation to others. Her sermons brought people to the altar, and she ministered to people through spiritual gifts. Various members of my family testified to being blessed by her ministry. In those early years, I assumed that women in all churches could minister from the pulpit and exercise their spiritual gifts among both men and women. I was not yet attuned to some of the limiting dynamics within the churches I knew and had yet to experience churches where women were not allowed to minister in that way. I would later learn that many churches did not allow this to happen, including some Pentecostal denominations.

Seeing my mother preach and teach significantly influenced me. For a number of years, she was the director of Sunday school and was the weekly Sunday school teacher for adults. These classes focused on teaching from particular books of the Bible or on a particular theme from the Bible. Beyond this, my mother has also been a preacher across the span of my lifetime. On numerous occasions, I witnessed her preaching to our congregation or as a guest preacher elsewhere. Almost always, her preaching would incorporate some form of ministry at the altar, where she and other church leaders would pray for seekers who accepted the invitation to come to the front. Some came forward to accept Jesus Christ as their savior, while others came forward for prayer. The gifts of the Spirit flowed during these times. In other words, it was commonplace for me to see my mother ministering to others and inviting them to experience the gifts of the Spirit.

Gendered expectations still contributed to how the gifts of the Spirit were experienced in the public worship of my church communities.[13] While men most typically preached from the pulpit and held positions of leadership, women were freer in exercising the gifts of the Spirit publicly at the altar and in less formal experiences.[14] On rare occasions, women broke through the order of service to share prophetic messages with the congregation. In one vivid incident, one hermana spoke a message exhorting the congregation to be ready for the return of Jesus Christ. It happened during a moment between worship songs when the congregation was experiencing heightened collective effervescence. She did not name a date for Jesus's return but more so emphasized the state of readiness that the congregation needed to remain in. She was a typically jovial woman who was very active in church activities, and I remember how, in this moment, she spoke up with a fervent authority, her voice unwavering in calling the congregation to a deeper expression of holiness.

An experience that especially stands out was when a woman recognized for operating in the gifts of the Spirit spoke a word of wisdom to me. My extended Calvillo family often organized worship services geared toward family and led by the numerous talented musicians in the family. The person ministering to the family at this particular worship service was a special guest whom I had never met, Sister Rachel. Someone in the family knew her through the network of churches that my family attended or ministered within. My spouse, Nani, and I arrived that evening to a warm and welcoming musical environment. There were about sixty people there, most of them related to me. The service began with various worship songs, mostly in English, as it was led by second- and third-generation family members who were bilingual and English-dominant. After an extended time of singing and praying led by the worship leader, the guest speaker was invited to speak from a podium. There was no stage or altar, and the speaker was level with the audience.

Sister Rachel came to the podium and began to share with the audience in a conversational manner. She spoke in a calm, authoritative tone, and her message emphasized how believers should follow the lead of the Holy Spirit. I recall that she illustrated the message by bringing someone from the audience to the front and having them act out what she was describing. The audience focused intently on her words, and some jotted down notes. The ambience shifted as she transitioned into what would become the altar call. Sister Rachel invited people whom specific aspects of her message had resonated with to come forward. The altar call was not a steady flow of people but rather a gradual flow coming forward with particular prayer requests. As Sister Rachel would pray for some and conclude her time with them, someone else would come forward to be prayed for. Her prayers, like her message, were steady and authoritative.

As the time of altar ministry pressed on, Nani and I spoke between ourselves and decided to go forward together. Something in the message had spoken to us, and we decided to let Sister Rachel pray for us. During that time, we were ministering alongside a local nonprofit organization in Santa Ana, California, and were essentially functioning as chaplains to neighborhoods with a significant percentage of immigrant families, many of whom were undocumented. Our ministry in Santa Ana was exhilarating and difficult. Nani was also employed as an elementary school teacher in the communities where we ministered.

Our moment of ministry in the Spirit with Sister Rachel began. We briefly introduced ourselves to her, providing little information about who we were or what we did. In the background, the music team played worship music, and many in the audience worshipped with their hands raised. She began to pray for God's guidance in our lives. As she prayed, she shifted into a more assertive tone. She had a word for us. She positioned her face close to us, between Nani and me, where we could both hear her clearly. She began to tell us that she saw us ministering in a neighborhood and that she specifically saw us gathered together with other people eating meals as a group. She did not see us in a church building but rather in some type of building that was next to apartments. She said she was not sure what those images meant to us but that whatever we were doing that related to those images, we should keep doing it. We were supposed to be there in this season, she assured us.

The tears streamed down our faces as she pronounced those words. We had been doubting whether we should remain at our ministry site in Santa Ana. We were ministering at a community center that was adjacent to rows of apartment buildings and spent a lot of time with people who lived in those apartments. One of the primary ministry activities was sharing meals together as a church. While the description she gave us was not lengthy or overly detailed, she mentioned various aspects of our ministry experience that were central to our community. I felt in that instant as if the Spirit had broken into our moment of self-doubt. We had doubted our place in the life of the community that we were committed to. Her words provided us with an instant infusion of encouragement. Through her prayers, we received a confirmation to keep going. We continued there for several years, deepening our connections to the community and our sense of kinship to the many friends we had there. That moment was pivotal.

A VULNERABLE POWER

Experiences of Spirit empowerment were central to Borderlands Pentecostalism. The promises of the Spirit offered Borderlands Pentecostals, as members of a minoritized community, a space to experience vulnerability and power that were inaccessible in other arenas. The spaces, moments, and events that surrounded these Spirit encounters were often times for us to consider who we were in the deepest sense possible. These were the moments of soul-searching when we hoped that God would see us for who we were and meet the desires of our hearts. Baptism in the Holy Spirit was an important point along this journey but not the endpoint. Rather, as we were baptized in the Spirit, we sought other gifts, other opportunities to minister to our communities and to uplift our peoples in ways that spoke to the realities of the day. Women often demonstrated authority through the gifts of the Spirit. Altars were instrumental in seeking these moments of empowerment and vulnerability. These altar moments often felt freer, less hierarchical, and powerfully collective as the Spirit empowered us together.

CHAPTER SIX

Unbounded Anointings

The song from the Christian Hip-Hop group SFC rattled the church sanctuary as my church friends and I performed our sound check for youth service. We had the sanctuary to ourselves before youth service started and played music typically not allowed in the church sanctuary. The song that captivated us that evening, which we played several times over, "In the House," released in 1992, resonated with our experience as young Latino Pentecostals. It was about receiving the baptism in the Holy Spirit. The artists described their experiences of empowerment and increased spiritual commitment after being baptized in the Spirit. Many in the youth group yearned to be baptized in the Spirit, and others had already had the experience and found affirmation in the song. For my peers and me, this song was anointed. It was anointed because it energized our spiritual strivings and enabled us to experience the active presence of God. Anointings, I came to recognize, sometimes showed up in unexpected places.

The concept of anointing in Borderlands Pentecostalism signaled a quality or state characteristic of certain people, moments, or creative acts that brought others closer to God in an experiential sense. Drawn from the concept in the Hebrew and Christian Scriptures of individuals being anointed with oil before taking on an important role,[1] anointing took on a broader spiritualized meaning in my context.[2] The Spirit gave certain anointings to people, particular capacities activated and enacted publicly for the good of others. Anointings could manifest through a ministry role but were more closely tied to spiritual gifts. When speaking of individuals, an anointing could be a reference to specific spiritual gifts exercised by a person, such as prophecy or interpreting tongues. Anointing could also refer to a collective moment when the presence of God was brought forth in a particular creative work that facilitated closeness to God, an urgency to know God, or a spontaneous clarity about God. "That service was anointed" or "That song was anointed," people might say. Anointing was a characteristic and quality of making God more accessible to others in a moment of palpable divine authority. Anointings could be long-term but also momentary, temporary, or situational.

In my experience, Hip Hop was anointed. I understood that some of this anointing came from key aspects of Hip Hop that resonated with and emanated from Black American church traditions.[3] I also observed how Hip-Hop artists spoke to people prophetically. They understood the context and the signs of the times and were able to captivate the hearts and minds of people through their music.[4] Though I recognized that many Hip-Hop artists communicated messages incompatible with what I learned at church, I sensed that even some "secular" or "worldly" artists were anointed. Their music was timely, and anointings had a timeliness to them, manifesting God's grace contextually. I experienced a draw toward this anointing that I felt in Hip Hop. It quickly became for me more than a cultural movement to observe and consume but rather one to create within.

A HIP-HOP PENTECOST

My initial connection to Hip Hop came through a teenager named Marcos, who came to live with my family for a year. Marcos was involved with popping, a dance style birthed in the Black American communities of Los Angeles, Central California, and the Bay Area. Often connected to funk music, this dance style took Latine communities by storm. Dedicated dancers found that dance could be an alternative to gang life; those who gained neighborhood fame for their dance skills often got a "pass" from local gangs and were allowed to move about without being threatened by neighborhood gangs. As Marcos navigated this neighborhood dance world, he found an alternative to gangs. In the process, he provided me with a vision of Hip Hop's power—its potential for anointing.

On a fateful day in 1984, I watched from a screen door as Marcos and his friends headed toward the elementary school at the end of our neighborhood block. I waited a minute, then darted off in that direction. As I ran along the sidewalk, I drew closer to a booming sound, an electronic-toned, fast-paced, thumping music with persistent synthesizer arrangements. The electro beat called to me. At six years old, I knew these rhythms from our neighborhood street; young men walked by blasting them on boom boxes, or vehicles cruised by, beats blaring. I reached a parking lot at the edge of the school property. There, a dozen or so young men of different ethno-racial backgrounds stretched and warmed up. Soon, some maneuvered over a checkered linoleum floor, spinning themselves over the smooth surface. These were b-boys. Others, poppers, contorted their limbs in robotic fashion. These distinct styles were coming together in what appeared to be a choreographed routine. What I witnessed was a Hip-Hop Pentecost. Young people of distinct racial backgrounds worked together and combined their talents for good. The moment stayed with me. It was an anointed moment.

In 1984, the prevalence of Hip Hop in my once white-majority working-class neighborhood signaled demographic shifts. At home, my Pentecostal Christian family only played Christian music, but that changed when Marcos arrived. Marcos previously lived about forty minutes away in the area known as the Inland Empire. That year, he enrolled at Buena Park High School a couple blocks away. In a recent conversation, he explained to me why he moved in with us:

There had always been a huge gang problem in the city [where I lived].
I fought it since I was ten years old. Two weeks before I moved in with
you guys, ten guys surrounded me, and one of them put a gun to my
head and pulled the trigger. The gun jammed and didn't go off. My older
brother made a decision that instead of all my brothers getting involved
and retaliating, he would move me away for a while. Three weeks after

this incident, this same gang member killed two rival gang members, and he has been in prison ever since.

Though Marcos was never an official gang member, dancing provided an alternative outlet to his penchant for confrontation. At his new high school, Marcos joined the Generation One Dance Crew, which competed in the neighborhood and at contests at Knott's Berry Farm amusement park.

The Pentecostalism I knew often maintained rigid boundaries between what was designated as sacred and profane while at the same time engaging in adaptive evangelistic and liturgical work that crossed sacred and profane boundaries.[5] One day I asked Marcos about his involvement with Hip-Hop dance: "Isn't that from the devil?" As a young child, I was echoing the language I had learned at church. As far as I knew, Hip Hop belonged in the realm of the profane.[6] At our church, we did not allow social dancing; neither did we listen to secular music.

Marcos listened to my question and paused. He then responded, "You know, dancing is exercise. It's good for the body." I thought about it as he walked away in his parachute pants, off to practice with his dance crew. I liked riding bikes and playing outside with friends, and I knew those activities were good for me. Why would dancing be different? Marcos's words challenged my young Pentecostal dichotomy of sacred and profane.

Anointings were often debated, and community members differed as to whether a person was truly anointed. On one occasion, a church member stood up to share a prophetic message with the congregation during a time of worship. The message was harsh in some ways, calling the congregation to a deeper commitment to God and exhorting them that they might miss out on God's presence. The brother who shared these words spoke with authority, then sat down. Church members differed as to whether his message had been truly anointed and commissioned by God. Some said it was what the church needed, while others found the message inappropriate, perhaps even self-aggrandizing. The perceived anointing for some was a miscalculated risk for others. I came to understand Hip Hop along these lines. Some Pentecostals did not see its anointing, but Pentecostals who identified with it received its anointing.

In the early '90s, members of my youth group at Las Buenas Nuevas in Norwalk, California, sought anointings with which to bless our communities and reach our peer groups. The youth group, like the larger congregation, was a place of convergence for people from working-class neighborhoods throughout the Los Angeles area. Among these teens, some were 1.5-generation youths in the process of acculturating to the US context. Others were second- or third-generation youths born in the United States to immigrant parents or even raised by immigrant grandparents. We were all finding our way in the US generational borderlands. We yearned to make the Holy Spirit real in our own lives and make Jesus real to others in ways that may not have been identical to our parents' and grandparents' experiences. The lyrics of one of our favorite youth-group worship songs captured this yearning: "Anointing fall on me." Even as we understood the potential for anointings to be far-reaching, we knew intuitively that anointings were contextual; anointings had to be legible within particular contexts to make an impact within those contexts. And sometimes, anointings legible to one generation were not legible to another. Hip Hop had a generational anointing.

EMBODIED ANOINTINGS

"Hey, so I started writing some rhymes," I said to my friends Julio and Cesar.

"Really? Me too!" Cesar responded. Julio, it turned out, had also been working on some lyrics. Julio was Guatemalan American and had grown up in Chicago for part of his life. Cesar was Costa Rican American and had lived for several years in Los Angeles County after his family migrated to the United States. The three of us had ended up in Fullerton, California, and attended the same church in Norwalk. The summer of 1993 was ending, and my friends and I embarked on a creative adventure. We concocted a string of verses together. The verses I wrote were about spiritual warfare, about fighting battles against the spiritual principalities that influenced the world around us. Julio and Cesar wrote a song about celebrating Jesus Christ as being risen and alive. We created two songs.

I had playfully dabbled in Hip-Hop rhymes in elementary school and junior high. A friend and I, in sixth grade, for example, ran for class president and vice president, respectively, and we wrote and performed a rap as a campaign ad. Even before that, I had watched a friend perform a rap song, "The Bible Break," in church. Hip Hop really took root in me when I watched a crew by the name of LPG perform at a youth camp in 1991. They were Dax and Jurny, two young Chicano rappers who combined an authoritative stage presence, energetic lyrics and vocals, and crowd-moving beats to share positive Christian messages. By then, I recognized that Hip Hop could be part worship, part outreach, part education, and part entertainment. If I could speak to the realities of the world through Hip-Hop rhymes, perhaps people would listen. In the summer of 1993, I prayed, asked God for empowerment, and began writing Hip-Hop lyrics. My friends had caught similar visions.

An aspect of being anointed for a task is the communal recognition of that particular anointing. My new Hip-Hop crew and I received affirmation and inspiration from two brothers, Tony and Caesar, who were themselves rappers. They were the younger brothers of Sister Sandy, a local evangelist who sometimes preached to our youth group. Sandy was anointed: her messages seemed to address directly what our young people needed to hear. On occasion, she would bring her two brothers with her, and they would perform for us, mixing rhymes and singing vocals with lyrics that encouraged young people to press on in their faith. We appreciated that Tony and Caesar were accessible to us and conversed with us after they performed. They and Sister Sandy listened to our stories and questions and responded with words of encouragement and challenge.

In the summer of 1993, my crew and I approached Tony and Caesar after they performed for our youth group. We shared that we were starting our own Hip-Hop group, and they were overjoyed. Tony and Caesar placed their hands on our shoulders and prayed for us, encouraged us to keep going, and gave us a few words of caution about pride. More than anything, they affirmed us. Then they came up with a name for us: Fully Armed Christians. Though the name was not necessarily what I would have come up with, it meant something because it was coming from these artists I respected. The name was likely based on an album from the group SFC, *Fully Armed*.

Our youth minister, Manuel, was there to witness these interactions, and he, too, encouraged us to keep working on our craft. To show his support, he offered us the opportunity to perform at a youth rally, where other church youth groups would be present. We could hardly contain ourselves. We would be ministering from the church stage, the altar itself. The following week, Julio, Cesar, and I met up at Cesar's house in Fullerton. We walked over to a local music store, probably a Warehouse Music, and picked out cassette tapes with "Whoomp There It Is," by Tag Team, and "Down with the King," by Run DMC. We practiced our lyrics over their instrumentals. We went to a local indoor swap meet in Anaheim, California. There, we paid an airbrush artist to paint some t-shirts that had our group's name emblazoned on the back.

On the Saturday night of our performance, we took to the stage with a mix of eagerness and hesitation. Cesar was an experienced dancer and seemed to be the most confident on stage. Julio had family there cheering him on and drew energy from that. I had family there, too, but came to the realization that this was a different type of performance for me. I had been in plays and had sung on stage, holding the mic many times, but this felt different. The performance went well. The crowd cheered for us with encouragement. We were met with smiles and applause. A church member commented to me, "You were great. You just need to learn to move on stage!" I took this as a challenge. If this was a real anointing, I needed to be fully present on stage.

We performed on a Saturday night, and on Sunday morning, the day after our performance, we felt ten feet tall walking into the church. For Sunday morning service, my friends and I sat toward the front. We looked toward the altar, the stage, which we had stood on the night prior. We sang several hymns and a few faster *coritos* that morning. Our church, Las Buenas Nuevas, was a very refined, classic Pentecostal church. Our pastors there were highly educated and very theological in their preaching and teaching. Our senior pastor at that time was well respected in our denomination, and I looked up to him.

Given our respect for our pastor, we were stunned by what he uttered that morning. Before introducing his sermon, he announced that our denomination was hosting its annual youth arts competition. He described the arts categories allowed in the competition. He then looked toward my group and said in a solemn tone, "What you boys did last night wouldn't qualify for any of the art categories allowed in the competition. It isn't art. You wouldn't be able to enter, boys." Then he proceeded to introduce his sermon. We had no knowledge of the competition, had not asked about any competitions, and it had not been promoted to our church previously. It felt as if he used the opportunity to tell us that Hip Hop was not art and was not recognized by the denomination. We glanced at each other with confused looks. We convened, regrouped, and decided we would keep going with our craft. If anything, I became more determined to continue. And I still respected our pastor. I just recognized that I was not writing rhymes for him.

CLEANSING LYRICS

Our Hip-Hop crew did not last as Julio, Cesar, and I became immersed in different activities at school. A year later, my family and I moved to a different church—back to El Buen Pastor—creating more distance in our crew, though our friendships remained. Our crew's momentum fizzled, but I continued to write rhymes and make other connections through my craft. In the three years that followed, I received invitations to share my gift at church services, youth group gatherings, and outreach events. These were all Pentecostal-based events. I soon had a repertoire of five or so songs that I performed publicly. I received affirmation at the church we now attended. When the pastor, Rev. Quintin Lazaro, heard me rap, I expected criticism. He was a thoughtful man, and when he said something positive to someone, he made it count. After I rapped at a youth service, he approached me, put his hand on my shoulder, and simply said, "¡Tremendo!" ["Tremendous!"]

In 1994, Pastor David of a church in East Los Angeles had seen me rap at a church youth service and invited me to perform at his church. Driving from our Fullerton home to East Los Angeles, I recall the consternation that I felt as my father and I stood on the cracked sidewalk, double-checking the church address I had scrawled on a crinkled sheet of paper. We looked around at the block of worn bungalow homes, and there was no church in sight, only a laundromat. The *lavanderia* sign was paired with what was the correct address. We walked into a bustling business, with customer demographics largely reflecting the Mexican American neighborhood of East Los Angeles. We asked some customers about the church and were pointed toward a back doorway, revealing a room with about two dozen folding chairs set up. This was the church.

Pastor David, who was setting up the chairs, greeted us with a bright smile and hearty handshakes. Once the rows were complete, he invited us to sit at the front. After some praying, a few praise songs, and some announcements, I was introduced before the fifteen or so older, working-class Latine attendees. Most attendees looked like they were showing up after a long day's work. I broke into my gospel rhymes imploring people to be cleansed of sin while customers washed their clothes a few feet away behind a partial wall. A small boom box played my cassette of recorded instrumental tracks. No microphone was needed in the cozy space. Before ending the service, Pastor David collected an offering. It turned out to be a "love offering," meaning it was gifted to me. I opened an envelope, revealing about fourteen dollars, including some change. I wondered if it was initially intended to be laundry money. Several of the attendees personally thanked me, including the owner of the laundromat. Though the audience was not a Hip-Hop crowd, I was grateful for the invitation and surprised to receive compensation for the first time in my life for rapping.

In those years, I led a double life. I was starting to enjoy the opportunities that came to me to rap at church outreach events, but I did not tell my school friends about this. At school, I was considered a nerd—and happily so. I was proud to be in honors classes. In those years at Buena Park High School, honors students typically stuck together because we were placed in the same classes together, filling up one classroom per grade. I also crossed over into athlete social circles as I played football for three years of high school. I wandered between the honors circle and the football circle. My football friends were tough, and I was not sure how my peers would think of me as a rapper. My honors friends knew me as a mostly reserved and shy, bookish peer. Not exactly the image of a rapper. I did share my skills with a handful of classmates, and they encouraged me to keep going.

ANOINTING IN UPRISINGS

I grew up hearing testimonies of people being delivered from lives of violence and gang conflicts, but those experiences seemed distant from my home life and my everyday lifeworld. In 1992, various events changed my understanding of the world. That was the year the Los Angeles uprisings took place. I sat glued to the television screen as an eighth grader, watching neighborhoods in Los Angeles go up in flames. The civil unrest was catalyzed by the acquittal of four police officers who had beaten Rodney King, a Black American man, in Los Angeles. The incident had been recorded on video and widely televised. The beating and the verdict uncovered other issues of inequality, injustice, and economic disinvestment that plagued some of the historically Black neighborhoods of Los Angeles. People were on edge and pushed over the edge due to the devaluing of Black life exhibited in the Rodney King trial.

Yet, even as the uprisings took place in communities largely outside of my neighborhood, the images I saw hit closer to home. The residents engaged in looting of local businesses included Latines. I discovered that someone I knew from my coethnic circles participated in this. The words of one man interviewed on television in Los Angeles amid the uprisings gripped me: "Rodney King could've been a Chicano." I understood that the devaluing of Black American lives was cause enough for unrest. But what I saw and heard helped me begin understanding the ways that race and place are intertwined, shaping people's chances in life. Likewise, I observed how distinct groups of peoples on the margins often deal with similar circumstances, sometimes in proactive coalition, sometimes in reluctant partnership, and sometimes through confrontation and competition for scarce resources. When I went to school in the days that followed, at a junior high with a significant Korean American population, I heard my classmates discuss the responses of Korean business owners. Some of my classmates had family in these Los Angeles neighborhoods. Tensions across minoritized racial groups forced me to think about how proximity across ethnic and racial lines did not automatically lead to solidarity. Smoke was in the air, and something had shifted in how I understood reality. I wondered about the anointings needed to engage these realities.

A few months later, I was off to high school at Buena Park High and focused on adapting to my new school with an increased attentiveness to the social realities around me. I quickly came to love my high school. I felt at home among my teachers and peers and became involved in a variety of activities on campus. I had attended a highly competitive junior high school in Fullerton Hills, where I was acutely aware of being from a different social class than most kids there. "You're not like the other Mexicans," some classmates told me; it was meant to be a compliment, but the comments began to sting. My high school was different. We had a sizable Latine population, as well as more substantial Southeast Asian, Black American, and white working-class student populations. Indeed, most of the white students at my high school lived in neighborhoods like mine, and some were more economically disadvantaged than I was. It was a diverse school where working-class diasporas converged.

A relatively affordable community minutes from the Los Angeles County line, my area became a landing place for working-class families moving out of Los Angeles County. Major population shifts occurred in the years following the Los Angeles uprisings. My diverse working-class community was an accessible option for some families leaving the Los Angeles area. As Black, brown, and Asian American households moved about the area, many young people made sense of their surroundings by claiming the neighborhoods they had come from, places where their extended families resided, or places they had ties to.[7] Young people were finding their way amid continued social dislocation. This happened across distinct ethnicities, from Pacific Islanders, to Asian Americans, to Black Americans, to Latines. In claiming neighborhoods, many implicitly or explicitly claimed the gangs that represented those neighborhoods. The school, which in the 1980s had been a majority-white one, rapidly became a majority-minority school.

In the 1994–5 school year, racial tensions flared up on campus. A 1998 *LA Times* article about my high school noted that in the mid-'90s, nearly half the student body felt unsafe there.[8] According to the article, some of these tensions were rooted in gang affiliations that students claimed; such affiliations were often racialized. Generally, my campus experience had been peaceful, but I did notice physical altercations becoming more frequent, and I sometimes tried to break up fights. With shifting demographics, notable tensions emerged between segments of Black American and brown Latino students. For several months during my junior year, Black-brown conflicts on campus ensued[9] among factions of the student body. The majority of students, from all ethno-racial backgrounds, were not involved in these conflicts. Many students crossed racial lines in their friendships and extracurricular activities; likewise some students did not easily fit within these Southern California racial categories, such as Afrolatines and those that had both Black American and Latine parents. Nonetheless, the ongoing tensions affected the student climate broadly. Nonstudents heightened these tensions, bringing particular street politics into campus activities after school, fanning the flames of conflict.

The conflicts escalated for me on one particular occasion when I got caught in the middle of a violent confrontation. From then on, I became reluctant to continue physically intervening in fights. I was shaken, sensing a spiritual oppression coming over the situation and feeling powerless as an individual. To me, this was spiritual warfare. I became active in various campus initiatives that worked toward peaceful solutions. For example, I joined a multi-racial conflict resolution program where I was trained as a mediator to help peers work on nonviolent solutions to conflicts. Our school sports teams also provided opportunities for collaboration and solidarity, even among some who had previously been in conflict with each other. As we competed with other schools, particularly wealthier suburban schools, we were all seen as kids from the hood, after all. The tensions slowly dissipated for a season, but I and other students of different backgrounds continued to wrestle with the fact that proximity did not automatically bring about solidarity across racial lines.

As I sought to make sense of what was happening in my surroundings, I found that Hip-Hop artists were speaking to these realities. Hip Hop took on a new meaning as a source of knowledge—an epistemology.[10] Chuck D of the group Public Enemy famously referred to Hip Hop as the "Black CNN." At that time, Los Angeles gangsta rap was going global. Simultaneously, Los Angeles had emerged as a hub of Latino Hip Hop, with a variety of brown creatives finding a platform in this musical genre to explain the realities of barrio life. These artists were anointed, perhaps not in the church but in a prophetic sense nonetheless. I recognized the power of Hip Hop. I did not agree with all Hip-Hop artists but recognized the potential for grassroots transformation that some artists, Christian and non-Christian, represented. I was especially interested in how Hip Hop could bridge racial divides and was drawn to grassroots, underground expressions engaged in this work of solidarity.[11] There was an anointing in the Hip-Hop zone,[12] a zone that I was increasingly devoting my time to.

RECOGNITION

When an anointing landed, I wanted to be ready to perceive it. On one special evening, the hype pulsated through my body. I had given a commencement speech as valedictorian for Buena Park High School's class of 1996; hours later, I was still on a natural high. That evening, I waited alongside my classmates in our school cafeteria for a bus that would take us to an overnight "grad-night" cruise in the Long Beach Harbor. I noticed a group of classmates who sustained their energy through creative expression. These classmates exuded collective effervescence as they configured themselves into a circle and coaxed each other into trading off rhymes over a beat. This was called a "cypher."[13] The vibrancy that disseminated from the small crowd of classmates was contagious. I made my way closer and could hear someone beatboxing, vocally producing simulations of kicks, snares, and high hats. Next to him, another student emitted rhymes, falling into the pocket of the beat. I saw that the emcee of the moment was one of our school's star basketball players. The group was multiethnic, but most active participants were Black Americans. From the outer edge, I pushed in, drawn by a centripetal force.

I squeezed toward the nucleus of the cypher, not to be a spectator but to be a participant. "I got something," I heard myself telling the group at the center. "Let him in," a few of the guys said. The beatbox transitioned to mimic a familiar beat, "Flava in Your Ear" by Craig Mac. The simulated horns and alternating kick-snare pattern floated overhead. I entered into a zone just as the beatboxer doubled up on the kick sound as if to set me up for an intro—pum, pa-pum, pa-pum, pa-pum. "These rhymes o-rig-inate from my mind / inspiration is divine / coming straight up with the gospel in a way that's not sublime." The rhymes poured forth in the valley of the beat, annunciated as I had done many times before, just never with a school crowd in this way. I had not yet finished my lines when the group erupted in pandemonium. I was pushed to and fro in the circle until the group started to fray. "Bring him back!" "Let him finish," some classmates exclaimed. The circle was reconstituted, and the same beat reinstated. I plunged into my rhymes again until I neared the end of the verse. Once again, my classmates pushed me around with glee. My affinity for rhyming throughout most of my high school years had remained a secret among most of my peers. I figured, *What better moment to share my pastime than now?*

The anointing enacted through conscious, mutual recognition in that moment stuck with me. As classmates slapped me on the back, extended hands, or reached out to bump fists, one classmate lingered and said, "That's some of that gospel rap" as he clasped his right hand onto mine and slid it off. Indeed, I had performed "gospel rap," a mainstay of my identity.

That cypher on my high school graduation night helped further my connection to Hip Hop. I had been writing rhymes, producing beats, and even performing at church youth group functions for about three years, but this took me into a more front-stage arena with my peers. More importantly, it solidified my own sense that Hip Hop, rooted in Black American freedom struggles and shaped in Afrodiasporic communities, could be grounds for solidarity across racial lines. I recognized that messages mattered within the art form, but what I came to realize was that the art of co-creation, the act of being in the cypher and being affirmed by the cypher, was a powerful experience. The cypher was anointed, and I had been allowed to partake of the anointing.

GENERATIONS OF ANOINTING

Despite some initial resistance, the Borderlands Pentecostal communities I knew became surprisingly open to Hip Hop, and by the late 1990s, I rarely encountered a pastor or leader who was opposed to it. I even discovered that many of the first churches to embrace Hip Hop were Latino Pentecostal churches that affirmed the anointing in this creative movement to work across racial lines. Likewise, as an arts movement originating within Black American communities, Hip Hop offered an opportunity to collaborate with and learn from Black American creatives to create spaces of resonance. Hip Hop became an important aspect of my crossing of ethnoracial lines. My commitment to solidarity with Black American and Afrodiasporic communities informs my engagement in the scene.

Hip Hop, like the Pentecostalism that was initially encountered by Mexican Americans in Los Angeles, draws foundational resources from Black spirituality. It is not surprising that I found such a strong resonance between Hip Hop and Pentecostalism. From Hip Hop, I learned that while anointings were highly contextual, they also had potential for drawing others into the cypher to experience divine goodness.

PART THREE

New Fronteras

CHAPTER SEVEN

Spaces of Resonance

"Be careful . . . they don't believe in the Holy Spirit there," a young Pentecostal evangelist cautioned me. I was enthusiastically speaking to him about my college selection as a senior in high school. Biola University in my Latino Pentecostal circles, I quickly learned, was rumored to be hostile to Pentecostal theologies and practices, though it was a nondenominational evangelical school.[1] I knew it was inaccurate to say that Biola did not "believe in the Holy Spirit," but I got a sense of what the evangelist was attempting to convey: "They believe differently than us when it comes to the Holy Spirit."

Because I planned to prepare for ministry, numerous church leaders in my circle opined about my college options. They were especially protective in relation to beliefs about the baptism in the Holy Spirit and the gifts of the Spirit. One trusted leader and family friend had a more positive opinion about my choice: "Biola is a great Christian university!" These conversations reflected how Latino Pentecostals theologically and institutionally negotiated their relationship to mainstream evangelicalism. The Latino Pentecostalism I knew negotiated between integration and differentiation when it came to white evangelicalism; they sought institutional integration into mainstream evangelicalism and integrated evangelical ideas and resources into their own religious worlds but also worked to maintain distinct Pentecostal practices and theologies. As Arlene Sanchez-Walsh notes, within the "larger evangelical world," Latino

Pentecostals "have carved out separate social, cultural, and religious spheres for themselves."[2]

As I was the first one in my immediate family to go to college, my faith tradition uniquely factored into my college selection process. College for many 1.5- and second-generation children of immigrants like myself has long been sold as a pathway toward upward mobility. While some find success outside of college, many working-class people of color perceive college as the best pathway for entering the middle class. Not only is college part of a credentialing process, but it also presents opportunities toward becoming more deeply embedded within social networks that reflect and bolster one's aspirations. Through the social capital accessible in these networks, college students and graduates find anything from job opportunities, to romantic partners, to hobby affinity groups. When a shared faith is part of the college experience, aspirations often move beyond career goals and into the realm of vocational discernment and spiritual growth. The social and educational experience becomes an opportunity to join a community of learners on a shared faith journey. For me, Christian higher education promised possibilities toward integrating, spiritually and socially, into a culture beyond my distinct Latino Pentecostal context. Yet, even in attending a Christian university, I knew the road was not determined for me. Perhaps I would remain embedded in Borderlands Pentecostalism, assimilate into white evangelicalism, or encounter something altogether different. As a committed student, I focused on my learning experience but had questions about the sense of belonging I would experience along the way.

CLOSE YET FAR: COLLEGE LIFE

I had initially avoided applying to Biola University for my own reasons: It was too close to home. It was only a fifteen-minute drive from home, with no freeway driving required. It was so close geographically to the life I already knew that I wondered if attending there would limit my growth. Yet several people I trusted recommended it. A member of my church, Sister Karen, was an alumna; the sole white member of our Latino congregation, Karen had a commitment to cross-cultural ministry and was fluent in Spanish. She spoke positively about her time at Biola. Likewise, several of my high school teachers recommended it, including one of the school's most beloved teachers, Mrs. Beth Swift, who attended Biola. I was especially intrigued by the prompting of my physics teacher, Mrs. Myra Philpott, who happened to be Jewish but recommended Biola for students looking into Christian higher education.

In the fall of my senior year, I finally visited Biola on a prospective students day. Once on campus, I felt the school was what I needed at that stage in my life. Having been accepted, I prayed, dialogued, and compared financial aid options with my family. I said yes to Biola.

With so much of my ethnic identity rooted in my faith community, I wondered about how aspects of my faith would be tested in this new setting. While looking at a public bulletin board filled with campus fliers, I noticed announcements for events from an array of ethnic clubs. I even saw an ad for a campus radio show that would be hosting several of my favorite Christian Hip-Hop artists live in studio. The culture was different from that of my own community, but I recognized spaces where I could connect. Furthermore, the proximity to my home would later turn out to be an important resource. I could share my community with others. I would remain a student at Biola for eight years, four as an undergraduate and four as a seminary student, all in a continuous stint.

Despite the university's proximity to my household, socially, it was worlds away. Biola was a majority-white school, and students largely represented affiliations to white-majority evangelical churches. Many had attended private Christian schools or grown up in communities with significant white evangelical populations. Many students came from suburbs wealthier than my own. Some had been homeschooled, and others had gone to international schools as children of missionaries, bringing a set of experiences distant from my own. Few were from local working-class neighborhoods or churches such as mine. Still, I established friendships with students representing all of these backgrounds and learned from them. I actually found myself more of an insider than I initially expected. Growing up in Orange County, I knew what it was to code switch and to adapt within majority-white spaces. Likewise, white-majority evangelical churches were never far in Orange County, and on occasion, I visited events hosted by such churches. I was familiar with white-majority evangelicalism.

In truth, mainstream white evangelicalism was familiar to my family. We drew from mainstream evangelicalism and adapted it to our needs. We also respected key leaders of the evangelical world, a practice connected to evangelical missions in Latin America. The label *evangelical* seemingly captured my identity as nearly all Latino Pentecostals in my circles self-identified with the evangelical cognate term *evangelico*.[3] Moreover, in some Latin American and US Latine contexts, *evangelico* was applied to most Protestants. *Evangelico* largely signified being Christian but not Catholic. Pentecostal commitments to evangelism and biblical inerrancy aligned well with evangelical commitments. Moreover, Latino Pentecostals are *evangelicos*/evangelicals in their faith and practice, with some caveats.[4] My time at Biola would test the overlap between the *evangelico* experience I knew and the majority-white evangelical experience I periodically observed.

BIBLICAL TEXTS AND CHRISTIAN CONTEXTS

I quickly discovered that chapel services would be an important part of my integration into the Biola community. Students were expected to fulfill a chapel attendance requirement. While some students complained about this, I found it to be a privilege. As much as some Pentecostals cautioned me about how Biola held different views regarding the Holy Spirit, the chapel services were comfortable to my Pentecostal tastes. The worship music was a major part of this reception for me. Rather than experiencing the setting as restrictive or not in tune with the Holy Spirit, I felt it a thoughtful, intentionally toned-down version of the revivalistic services I knew. Sure, the Spanish *coritos* were missing, but I was familiar with the music that was played and eagerly learned new songs. This was a space tailored to people at my stage of life, students who were seeking purpose and connection. As I looked around during the chapel services offered at orientation week, for example, I observed students who were in awe of God. Many raised their hands as they worshipped, a practice I associated with Pentecostalism. The sense of surrender I was used to at youth camps and services was also present here.

The treatment of the Bible at Biola, particularly through preaching and within my Bible classes, intrigued me. In my communities, we understood the Bible as inspired by the Holy Spirit and authoritative for the way we lived; so far, these views resonated with what was taught at Biola. In my church world, though, these presuppositions showed up differently than at Biola: preachers would preach to provoke action, not merely in the aftermath of the sermon but also often during the sermon. The posture of the Latino Pentecostalism I knew was to inspire people to respond to God in the here and now, often amid the sermon or during the altar call following it. Sermons often integrated testimonios and other narrative genres, call-and-response practices, and passionate intonations from the preacher. Furthermore, in the borderlands, people often came to the sermon time with present and pressing needs; Borderlands Pentecostals expected sermons to address their needs and sought to respond urgently at the altar. Teaching was meant to prepare one to preach in the borderlands.

The Bible practices I was familiar with had significantly shaped my relationship to the Bible, and at Biola, I began to rethink the place of the Bible within the art of preaching. At Biola, the biblical text was scrutinized and analyzed in ways that were new to me. Often, sermons included verse-by-verse analyses within particular passages. Indeed, the university taught students to most value expository preaching, which was bibliocentric, focused on the meaning of the words in the text. In the expository preaching modeled for us at Biola, much of the emphasis was on understanding the historical context of the text. I was taught to delve into the culture of the original audience whom the text was written for, to inquire about the historical events that led up to the text we were reading, and to learn the original languages of the texts.

To be clear, some of the Pentecostal pastors and preachers I had been exposed to were dedicated to biblical exposition. The two most recent pastors I had leading up to college were both Latino Pentecostals with seminary educations. One had a doctorate. They often dove into the historical contexts of texts and exegeted the original languages of the texts. My mother was also a dedicated Bible teacher who spent hours reading the text and studying commentaries. Still, what I observed at Biola was a culture that held up the written word in an authoritative way that I was not used to. The authority that I knew manifested as people responded to the text. Authority was something Pentecostals saw and experienced outwardly; we felt it not necessarily in a way disconnected from the intellect but in a way that required us to be bodily present. At college, the text itself was the authority as the written word of God. The sense I began to gain in college was that I could know the word—and the will—of God by studying the text. It was not enough to merely memorize the Bible or to read it regularly, practices that were commonplace in the Pentecostal churches I knew; rather, it was important to exegete the text through hours of study. I later became aware of Pentecostal scholars who did this type of work as well, but for the time being, I romanticized this as a "new" approach for me.

My newfound discipline for the study of the text cut into my Pentecostal presuppositions in unexpected ways. Within some of my theology classes, I encountered professors who questioned particular Christian leaders who were valued within my circles. For example, I recall one professor who spent time discrediting the teachings of prosperity gospel and word-of-faith preachers. I already had serious doubts about prosperity gospel preachers who were famous in the mid-1990s. However, many of these preachers, authors, and pastors occupied space within the religious ecology of Latino Pentecostalism. Preachers frequently featured on the Trinity Broadcasting Network, for example, were largely from Pentecostal backgrounds themselves, and many, though not all, embraced prosperity gospel and word-of-faith theology. These were "name it and claim it" type of theologies. Several professors I encountered cast doubt on the Christian faith of these preachers, primarily based on their approach to biblical exegesis, identifying some as heretics and false teachers.

I entered a crisis of faith. The plausibility structure[5] that held up my faith was being challenged. People whom I understood as bolstering the faith life of my community were being questioned in ways I was not used to. It was difficult for me to simply cast people out of the fold based on the particular theological disagreements put forth. These were preachers who, though I disagreed with their teachings, were still part of the Pentecostal family that I knew. I still saw them as being part of my spiritual family. I knew people whom had been ministered to by these preachers, some who perhaps pointed to an experience they had at a church service led by one of these preachers as an important milestone in their spiritual journey. I knew many who testified to experiencing the Holy Spirit through one of these preachers. Furthermore, aside from these big-name preachers, I knew local pastors, preachers, and family members who subscribed to some of the theologies of these faith teachers. We could have in-house disagreements in our local churches, but declaring preachers to be non-Christians challenged me. It had long made sense to me that wrong teachings and heresy existed, but it was difficult for me to simply cast away people who had contributed to the communities I knew.

I began to question aspects of the Pentecostalism I knew. I held on to aspects of the experiential expectations I learned through Pentecostalism but in highly tempered ways. It was no longer acceptable to simply let myself go in worship, for example. The notion of surrender became less and less feasible in the way I had previously known. Certainly, I could surrender myself to God and could experience emotion while worshipping, but always under control. During this time, I continued to attend my family's Latino Pentecostal church, but I became more judgmental about the theology espoused at the church. I was especially critical of the experiential aspects of the tradition. Altar ministry seemed less necessary as it was really through the preaching of the word that lives were changed. I found myself analyzing many of the sermons I sat in on and critiquing the ways meanings were read into the text rather than being drawn from the text. The hermeneutics were often wrong, I thought to myself. It became difficult for me to simply sit through a sermon at my family's church, even though I continued to love the people who were part of my spiritual family. In fact, through all these years, I continued to serve at my church. I taught Sunday school for children and at times taught youth classes. I even preached my first full sermon at my church during my second year of college.

I wandered for a season in a spiritual borderlands[6] of sorts, having a love for the spiritual communities where I came from but finding a different way of approaching spiritual growth. I took several steps to alleviate the cognitive dissonance I felt as I questioned some of the practices of my church and delved into a new relationship with the Bible. The methods of spiritual vitality were largely to be found in the correct exegesis of the Bible. Through my college years and, later, seminary, I began to translate within my Latino Pentecostal church setting many of the concepts I was learning at school. Generally, my teachings were well received. I focused more on the methods of biblical interpretation and less on calling people out if their particular theology did not match what I learned at school. Still, at the time, I figured that if people could learn the "correct" way of reading and interpreting the Bible, they would figure out the truth for themselves.

I found some respite in the principles I learned from intercultural studies courses; these courses focused on contextualizing theologies within diverse contexts. My *evangelico* and Borderlands Pentecostal ties sustained a desire to remain grounded in my communities. Pentecostal and charismatic classmates I met along the way served as encouraging conversation partners. A scholar of the book of Acts, Dr. Harold Dollar served as my academic mentor and offered theological frameworks for crossing social boundaries. Though he did not use the term "borderlands," the resonance was there. I continued to engage in my community back home but also discovered I needed community at school to keep me grounded.

FINDING COMMUNITY

Recognizing my need for consistent community on campus significantly improved my experience. Certainly, a part of my college experience was highly introspective and individually focused. I had learned to be disciplined at my schoolwork early on in life, and since I continued to have contact with my family and church family, I had community outside of campus. On campus, I began to connect with members of different ethnic clubs. Fortuitously, the presidents of the Korean American and Filipino American student associations lived several doors down from me in the dorms. I became busy visiting different ethnic student associations and felt welcomed at all of them. What I discovered is that many of the members of the different ethnic student associations showed solidarity across distinct ethnic student associations. Many white allies were also active participants, some having lived in other parts of the world or in diverse neighborhoods. Multiethnic support among students was at a high point when I arrived on campus, and having come from a diverse, multiethnic high school, I felt this mattered.

One of the most important spaces I experienced at Biola was Unidos, the Latino student association on campus. Some of my closest, most supportive friendships were formed through this organization. By my second year, I joined the leadership. In my prior stage of education, I had thought of ethnic clubs as spaces for students who were acculturating to the US context and perhaps learning English. In college, I learned it had less to do with language and more to do with building community and empowerment and creating opportunities for others to experience our cultures. Ironically, I came to embrace my Spanish fluency more fully there. I had been given the gift through my home and church life of being bilingual and now drew from that resource at college. During my time at Biola, I had no Latine professors. Meeting scholars and leaders through Unidos became important. And above all, my peers within Unidos affirmed many of the experiences I'd had through their own experiences.

I was excited to learn during my first semester that our Unidos group would be leading one of the all-campus chapel services for Hispanic Heritage Month. This would be an opportunity to showcase our culture through a worship experience. Since I had experience singing on worship teams in my Pentecostal church, I was asked to join a student worship team that we put together for chapel. Our group planned to sing bilingually a set of songs that we sang at our Spanish-speaking churches, inviting the campus to join us. Several of the members of the team were from Pentecostal churches similar to mine. That morning, the school gym, where our chapels were held, was filled to capacity. We dressed nicely, as we would for church, hoping to present an image of what the worship experience was for us. The chapel opened with our team leading worship, and since we were the first component that students experienced that morning, I felt nervous. Other than a slight technical difficulty with our keyboard synthesizer, our set went smoothly, and we were able to get through our songs as planned. I was especially pleased with how our last song landed, a mostly acapella harmonizing of the phrase *unidos venceremos*, followed by the translation, "united we shall overcome." I walked away feeling satisfied with the experience we had led our student body through.

I soon learned that not all students were happy about our chapel. Our university had developed a helpful campus intranet service that many students used to communicate and build affinity groups. The intranet system, called BUBBS, allowed students to sell items on campus, discuss courses, debate topics of interest such as theology, and dialogue about campus issues. Conversations were organized in online forums situated within folder icons. One particular folder discussing our weekly chapel services drew conversation about our particular service. Several students complained via forum posts about the notion that an ethnic-specific chapel was not conducive to student unity but rather sowed division. If chapel was about worshipping Jesus Christ, and we were all followers of Jesus, some reasoned, why would it be of benefit to allow an ethnic-specific group to share its culture with the larger body? Though our worship session had been bilingual and had included translations, there were times when we led the group in Spanish-language songs. For some students, this experience was alienating rather than enriching. Others complained about the Latino speaker who had shared during chapel that day. The message he shared had been primarily autobiographical rather than an expository sermon.

I did not expect to experience this type of resistance in relation to our chapel service.[7] For me, it had been a celebratory occasion. It was disheartening to think some students saw our shared Christian faith as grounds for speaking against diversity, as if our very presence and affirmation of our ethnic identity in relation to our Christian identity had been offensive to them. In the coming months, I learned there was a contingent of students on campus who regularly responded this way to issues of diversity, equity, and inclusion. These students appealed to the Christian faith as a grounds for not addressing issues of diversity and justice. The Christian faith was seen as washing over collective sins of racial injustice rather than as grounds for engaging these issues and making things right. A colorblind approach was the go-to discourse that many students employed in this context, asserting that since we were all the same in Christ, we did not need to emphasize those aspects that made us unique ethnically, let alone issues of systemic inequality and injustice.[8] I did not give up on the school because there was enough support from a diverse community of students, faculty, and administrators, including some white allies. We had a community worth struggling for, I thought, and so we continued to build.

CONVERGING CULTURES

In moments when my community and culture were questioned, I was grateful for the space and resources developed by one particular mentor on campus, Glen Kinoshita, who directed the multiethnic programs at Biola. He mentored and supervised student leaders, directed a scholarship program for ethnic minorities, organized events that resourced students, held retreats for multiethnic students, and was simply there to listen to and encourage us. Glen's firm yet nurturing spirit helped me understand issues of structural inequality and social justice, and he likewise introduced me to theologies that represented a wide array of peoples within the Christian community. Moreover, he helped us theologize about diversity. Diversity was not merely a problem to be solved or worked through; it was a preferred reality that helped us better understand who God was. This resonated with my Pentecostal sensibilities that looked to the church in Acts chapter 2 as a model for how faith in Christ could break down walls of difference while maintaining a sense of diversity.

Within our multiethnic programs community, we often had difficult conversations related to racial justice. I remember one theme that periodically emerged: the representation of Jesus Christ in a mural on campus. This mural, a centerpiece of art near our campus cafeteria, depicted a Jesus of fairer skin and white European features despite the artist, Kenneth Twitchell, avowing that the model for the image was a Jewish man. Nevertheless, for many students of color, the image communicated a presupposition held by many evangelicals that Jesus looked like a white man. I realized I had internalized such an image of Jesus Christ as a white man. I especially learned from my Black American peers about how such images shaped our theology and the way we related to God. At times, our conversations turned to discussions about some of the conflicts within and among peoples of color. These were important conversations for me to work through and helped me find hope after experiencing conflict among students of color in my younger years. One formative annual event, the Student Congress on Racial Reconciliation, brought together students from an array of Christian colleges to discuss issues of racial justice and Christian theology. These were some of the most life-giving times I experienced on campus.

Something I held on to closely when I arrived at Biola was my connection to Hip-Hop culture. For me and various other Hip-Hop heads on campus, Hip-Hop became an alternative space of creativity. Some of us performed together, wrote songs, produced beats, and at times freestyled together. We also explored the burgeoning Hip-Hop scene in the greater Los Angeles area together. At the time, a unique phenomenon was taking place in the region wherein some Christian

Hip-Hop artists were participating in the local underground Hip-Hop scene, which was not explicitly Christian. Some of these Christian artists even hosted events at their own venues, blurring the boundaries between underground Hip Hop and Christian Hip Hop. Many of these artists were themselves Latino Pentecostals, and some Hip-Hop events were hosted at Latino Pentecostal churches. In this season, Hip Hop became a platform where my Latino Pentecostal identity came through in ways that it did not elsewhere. Furthermore, the communities we built there significantly influenced the way I understood the boundaries between the sacred and the profane. What had once been a rigid delineation became a borderlands. I found myself in conversation with the world of underground Hip Hop as I made sense of the racialized realities around me. I appreciated the spaces of worship that Biola offered me, but these Hip-Hop spaces also became crucial sites of spiritual connection.

Two important outgrowths of our Hip-Hop community work emerged: The university institutionalized an annual Hip-Hop concert, and I joined a newly formed Hip-Hop crew. Through the administrative advocacy of a friend, Liza, an annual Hip-Hop concert called Sola Soul became a funded event at Biola. Here, the Hip-Hop elements of graffiti, breaking, DJing, and emceeing were showcased. The event would draw a variety of visitors who would rarely visit our school, alongside campus participants hungry for this type of expression. Our events platformed many of the local artists who occupied borderlands between underground and Christian Hip-Hop—artists like Click the Supah Latin, Propaganda, I.D.O.L. King, Deviance, LA Symphony, Ahmad Jones, and others. We also opened the stage for our campus talent. On numerous occasions, I got to emcee the event and sometimes performed my own sets as well. An offshoot of our Hip-Hop concerts was the launching of an ongoing spoken-word poetry lounge. Through our Hip-Hop organizing, we created alternative spaces on campus that centered a Black American–birthed, Afrodiasporic movement and held special meaning for brown creatives like myself.

At these events, I became acquainted with another emcee, Gio, and a DJ, Jason. Gio, Jason, and I formed the first iteration of Homestyle, a multiracial Hip-Hop unit that performed throughout the Los Angeles basin. We were considered an underground, or alternative, Hip-Hop crew with a Christian message. Many of the gigs we got invited to were church youth-group events, as well as coffee shop events and outdoor neighborhood festivals. Our audiences included ethnically diverse crowds, majority–Asian American audiences, Latine-majority groups, Black-majority venues, and white-majority events. For about two years with Homestyle, I experienced a great slice of the greater Los Angeles area. In this season, we collaborated with other local artists and helped boost the scene in the region. As an artist, my commitment was largely to community-building and establishing resonance with others through the co-creation of art.

Through my involvement in this Hip-Hop work, I met another special person, Puanani Rosario Poti. She was a leader within the multiethnic programs at Biola. At one of our concerts, we were introduced to each other, and I was drawn to the ways she brought others into community. We had many mutual friends, and she was even related to a friend of mine from high school. Her connections to her Filipino American and Samoan roots represented an important source of spiritual nourishment in her life. As we continued to collaborate within our multiethnic community, we were drawn together. We committed to building together a community of healing centered on our Christian faith and drawing from our convergence of brown diasporas. We continue to explore the ways the Spirit moves through the centers and edges of our cultures.

BORDERLANDS CONSCIOUSNESS

When thinking of my experience in Evangelical higher education, I found resonance in the concept of double consciousness proposed by W. E. B. DuBois.[9] The concept specifically describes the experience of Black Americans working to remain true to their communities but also attending to and confronting the demands of white society. I wanted to honor the specificity of DuBois's concept in speaking to the experience of Black Americans. At the same time, I noticed parallels in how some Latines recognize that their experiences are on the periphery of a particular institutional context. Often, those on the margins are expected to assimilate. And many on the margins feel a sense of commitment to their own communities. We often hold on to our communities and to the resonances thereof while seeking ways to succeed within the institutional systems before us. Some are not allowed to belong, at least not in their full selves. I think of some of the Queer students I met on my journey who hid their identities from the institution even as they contributed to community life. Biola became home for me as I encountered people and resources that allowed me to express the spiritual resonances I embodied.

It was of utmost importance for me to help build spaces of resonance within the institutional context in order to find my own sense of purpose and spiritual formation. While I experienced a time when I considered completely buying into institutional expectations, I quickly recognized there were aspects of myself that I was not willing to give up. For a time, I compartmentalized aspects of who I was. I was deeply committed to the study of the Bible, for example, poring over commentaries, mastering the original languages, and learning to outline my own interpretations and readings of the text. And yet I was likewise committed to the Borderlands Pentecostal communities I came from. Building community through Unidos, multiethnic programs, and Hip Hop provided a creative resonant space wherein I worked out some of the incongruent aspects of the worlds I moved through. In these creative multiethnic spaces, I found room to theologize, and to encounter the divine, while working out questions, doubts, motivations, and conflicts. Rather than assimilating and rather than retreating, I found spaces of cross-ethnic resonance that affirmed the beauty in our differences. The resonance of the Spirit became ever more real during this season as I found home in niches of multi-ethnic, urban, and justice-oriented expressions of evangelicalism.

CHAPTER EIGHT

El Llamado

"You better not do that to me, God," I prayed as I rode in the back of my parents' station wagon on a Sunday evening after church. A guest preacher had shared about how God had "called" him to the ministry to be an itinerant evangelist, preaching at different churches and earning a living from that. I dreaded the idea that God would call me to the ministry. In my church community, people spoke about *llamados*, or callings. This was the notion that certain people were designated for the Lord's work, set apart to lead others toward a closer, more committed life with God.[1] Being called was supernatural as it came from the Holy Spirit, but it was a natural part of my church community. People experienced callings, and the community needed called people in order to operate. To be called, as I understood it then, was to fulfill a role labeled as ministry, typically as a pastor or an evangelist. Subsisting from a calling, as I observed, meant either living on a pastor's salary paid by working-class congregants or receiving inconsistent pay as an evangelist traveling from church to church. None of this appealed to me.

During the evening service, when the minister explained that God provided for him through offerings and other funds that he received ministering at disparate churches, I thought about how his was a life of faith, reliant on someone else's provision. I didn't want that. It didn't match my goals. My dream went as far as the hills. In my hometown, the working-class neighborhood that we lived in was a few blocks from the freeways and consisted of single-family homes and apartment units. I was privileged enough to live in a house, but I could see the hill neighborhoods of the city and dreamed of living in a mansion there. Conversely, people called to ministry had to be obedient in whatever God called them to do, even if that meant living in scarcity.

"That's not what I want, God. Don't you dare call me to that kind of life, God," I firmly prayed in the car that evening. Rarely did I pray with this tone.

BORDERLANDS CALLING

A few years later, when I was fifteen, my youth pastor at Las Buenas Nuevas announced to our youth group a special opportunity. A group of churches from our denomination organized a spring break short-term mission trip to Tijuana, Mexico, for youth groups. Participating youth groups were from Northern California churches. As our youth pastor explained, Latine churches like ours had the opportunity to partner with these white-majority churches and go on a mission trip as Spanish-language interpreters. The youth groups would run children's programs at churches in Tijuana and would work with congregations in hosting other church services.

The mission trip opportunity intrigued me. I'd already translated for my parents and other family members and taught children's classes at church, even as a young teen. I could translate for a group of teens in Mexico. I signed up along with a handful of other friends and was assigned to a group from the town of Susanville, California. When spring break came, we drove down to San Diego, where we gathered with hundreds of other teens. As I had expected, most of the youth groups were overwhelmingly white. There were a few groups from Oakland and other Bay Area cities that were diverse, but most were not. We met our assigned group that evening, and the next day we would be bused across the border to be dropped off at our church sites. My friends and I were shy and cautious about what to expect.

Our mission team was housed by a local Assemblies of God church in Tijuana, and we worked with the children of the church for several days. We also helped host several evangelistic services at the church and at a mission church in a newer, less developed neighborhood. We were also allowed to venture into the neighborhood for short walks, such as to buy snacks at local markets. We built few in-depth relationships with the people of the local church. The connections we established were largely within the mission team. It was an experience of cultural adjustment for the team and, to some extent, for my youth-group friends and me as well. As I have often heard in critiques of short-term missions, our trip largely focused on the young people participating and less on the communities being "served." I do believe that many of the leaders and participants were sincere in their desire to do something positive for the communities they were visiting, but the types of activities were short-term in their scope.

The mission trip was a pivotal experience for me. I was there to serve, and my experience in serving allowed me to exercise leadership in various ways. I had already been in leadership positions with my church, but here, the experience of leadership through translation was especially life-changing. I began to understand that I was not only there to translate language, but I was also there to bridge cultures. I was there to make sense of the experience for white Americans and to also make these white Americans intelligible to the local Mexican community. What I discovered is that I was not just a translation machine or a dictionary; I was a mediator, and my presence made a difference. I could influence the quality of the experiences that others were having.

Because I was so driven by my sense of mission, I understood my role as going beyond interpreter and tour guide. I was there to make the gospel understandable to people. As an interpreter, I had to listen, ask questions, be aware of my surroundings, and observe how people moved and operated in their settings. Through it all, I needed to be in tune with the Spirit. Truth be told, I was learning about the local community myself. Initially, I was surprised to find that many people in Tijuana already had the ability to translate between English and Spanish. At various points, members of the church were able to step up and translate for the congregation. Many locals lived a borderlands reality of being bilingual and bicultural. Some had already lived and/or worked in the United States. The locals likely could have done the translation work without us. Yet my role was more relational than mechanical.

For the week, I became immersed in multiple worlds: in the lives of these white teens from a small town in Northern California and in the Tijuana neighborhood where we stayed. Bridging these worlds was a creative experience. I was guiding locals and the mission team through experiences of understanding each other. On several occasions, I had to deal with conflicts in the team. There were misunderstandings with the church leadership but also misunderstandings between some of my own church friends and the youth group we were assigned to. I realized that the way that I distilled my own knowledge and stories to make sense to people across contexts mattered. I also discovered that the context in Tijuana was not completely foreign to me. My times visiting churches in the borderlands as I grew up made the experience familiar. I could especially connect to the practices, the hymnody, and the preaching of the Pentecostal church there. In some ways, the neighborhood church in Tijuana felt like home. A few years later, I even discovered that the pastor of that church was related to some family friends, pointing to the ways that my peoples were connected across borders.

ACCEPTANCE

Though there was not a rigid formula, the experience of being called—that is, the moment of knowing one was called—was also something I wondered about as a preteen after that Sunday evening service. How did ministers, like the preacher from that Sunday evening, know they were called? Calling was often talked about as something that people just knew deep down—something that the Spirit affirmed in people. Accepting a calling, as people described it, was like recognizing something about oneself that made sense. People might run from their calling and experience turmoil, but there was peace in accepting a calling. And at some point, there would be confirmations of this calling. It might come as a prophetic word that a gifted speaker would direct at a person, for example. It could also come through a mentor or leader who saw particular gifts in a person. And as callings became more public, confirmation would often come from the broader congregation celebrating a person's calling. "Tiene llamado!" the hermanas and hermanos might say. Calling then was felt internally, confirmed by gifted observers and affirmed by the broader community.

It was during the week in Tijuana that I received my calling. El llamado occurred. Somewhere amid the interpreting, the working with children, the resolving conflicts, and the speaking to pastors and leaders in Tijuana, something clicked. It was as if a light went on inside me. The roles I took on, the skills that I needed to work effectively, seemed to point to my possibilities in ministry. I admitted to myself that I had a calling to ministry, and life seemed to make sense. "I really am called to the ministry," I told myself. Somehow, the thoughts I had previously found revolting had dissipated. The Spirit stilled my doubts and gave me peace.

I returned home from this trip and immediately told my parents that I had been called to the ministry. They embraced me with joy. To be called was something that was cause for celebration for them. They had been careful not to push me in that direction, as I would later find out. They never directly told me to seek out a ministry calling, yet they shaped the context wherein the vision for a calling was born. They helped set the stage. Now, as I had shared my awakening sense with them, they affirmed me. They shared with other family members that I had received a calling. They did not proclaim it publicly, but others close to them knew. Over time, this would open up conversations about my future trajectory, about what preparation looked like, about the life decisions I would be making in the coming years. But for now, it was a time of embrace and a time of affirmation. Others in my extended family affirmed my calling. I especially remember my tías congratulating me and my grandmothers, Adelina and Josefina, affirming that they were praying for me.

For a high school freshman, though, more pressing was my strategizing about how much I could reveal to my friends about being called. I was especially bonding with my sports teammates, with whom I spent several hours a day training and competing. I decided to finish off the school year and not talk about my sense of calling with my friends. When the new school year began that fall, my sophomore year, I decided I would share with more friends what it meant for me to be called. I didn't use the language of *calling*, but I talked about what I planned to do with my life after graduation. Slowly, I began to share with my friends that I would study to become a minister after high school.

As my tenth-grade football season got underway, I volunteered to pray before our first game of the season, as our team typically prayed before games. My teammates seemed to like my prayer. Some of them, by then, knew I was planning to go into the ministry as a career. Because I was Mexican American, a rumor spread among team members that I was going to be a Roman Catholic priest. The nickname Father Calvillo stuck with me for that year and spread beyond the football team. When it came time to pray, the teammates called on me. Early on, before I had become the permanent prayer person, another teammate filled in. The team did not appreciate his prayer because he said, "God, help us to kick their asses." One teammate called out, "Let's get Father Calvillo next time!" Thus the name, the role, and the rumor were solidified. For several months, sporadically, classmates would approach me with the question, "Do you really wanna be a priest?" I would explain to them that I wanted to be a minister but not a priest because I wasn't Roman Catholic.

People seemed to accept my plans to go into the ministry, even if they didn't understand why I wanted to do it. Teachers started to inquire about it as well. I began to receive advice about some of the Christian universities that I might consider. I amassed a list of potential schools, and all were within the evangelical tradition: Azusa Pacific, Biola, Vanguard, Westmont. These were all schools in my vicinity. I even considered one school that was farther away, Wheaton, as I was told it was the "Harvard of Christian universities." Yet I soon realized I didn't want to go far. I wanted to excel academically and to remain connected to my community. It was difficult for me to envision serving communities farther away. And being from a sprawling region like Southern California, I figured everything I could ever want was at my fingertips.

COLLEGE CALLING

When I graduated from high school, I headed to Biola University for my undergraduate studies. There was a number of resources I encountered at Biola that continued to shape my sense of calling. In fact, it was during my time at Biola that my sense of calling took another major turn. During my first week there, I met several students who had participated in a summer internship program based out of a para-church ministry in Santa Ana, California. The organization, called Hispanic Ministry Center, ran a summer program called Kidworks, in which college students lived in majority-Latine communities in or around Santa Ana and ran summer programs for children, teens, and families. It did not sound like the in-house ministry approach I was used to from my family's churches, but I was drawn to the idea of serving in an urban ministry setting.

During my second college semester, I attended Biola University's missions conference, an annual event that brought together mission organizations both local and from around the world, including Hispanic Ministry Center, and platformed speakers engaged in cross-cultural ministry work. I got to meet Larry Acosta, the cofounder of the Hispanic Ministry Center, and he shared with students at several conference sessions about how he grew up in a working-class neighborhood in Santa Maria, California, raised by a father who once worked in agriculture and a mother who was orphaned at a young age. He shared from his own life and talked about how God sometimes called people to serve in communities beyond those they are familiar with. His *testimonio* was interwoven into the challenge that he put forth to the students about doing ministry in cross-cultural settings. A portion of his message especially resonated with me:

As a person of color, you feel this major need to prove to the world that you're not a nobody, and so, why would you ever go to a little school like Biola and go into the ministry? Because in a real crude sense, that doesn't really matter in the world's eyes. How are you going to prove to the world as a person of color that you made it that you have worth and value by going that route? And in a very honest way, those were some of the struggles that I had. Because I felt pressure to prove to the world that I was not a nobody. And I began to wrestle with God, and I had this wrestling match going on.[2]

Larry's words hit close to home for me because I had internalized a particular notion of success that was in conflict with my sense of calling to ministry. I was the son of immigrants. I wanted to succeed beyond how my parents had succeeded. I wanted to give back to them for all they had done for me. Living in Orange County, I had also seen what some of my wealthier peers had access to—the types of resources, networks, and experiences that came with upward mobility. And as I excelled at school early on and worked hard to earn my grades, I wondered why I would not also deserve some of these benefits. Furthermore, as a brown-skinned Mexican American student, I rarely saw students who looked like me succeeding in higher education. I wanted to break stereotypes and show the world that we could succeed. When I entered the classroom, I often felt I needed to prove to others that people like me had something to contribute. Whenever I opened my mouth in the classroom, I felt I needed to make my people proud.

In my mind, I reconciled my dreams of wealth and success with my call to ministry by telling myself I would someday be the pastor of a wealthy church. I thought of some of the churches up in the hills that I drove by in my neighborhood as a preteen. I thought that perhaps I could someday prove myself to be an effective pastor who would be called to a "successful" church ministry. If I had accepted a calling to the ministry, at least I could be placed at a church that would allow me to live the way that I had hoped. I would have a church on the hill and a house on the hill, I told myself. Never mind that this would take me away from many of the communities that I came from. I figured that would all be worked out somehow.

TRANSFORMATION

If meeting peers who participated in the Kidworks summer program piqued my interest, hearing and meeting Larry Acosta energized me to try out the program. In the summer after my freshman year in college, I participated in an internship program that involved living in a community where a team of college students and I ran programs for kids and teens. Santa Ana, California, became a special place to me. I had visited Santa Ana countless times before as it was a hub of the Latine community in the region. I had grown up visiting several churches in Santa Ana for special events. This time, I would have a different experience of the city.

The neighborhoods we served in Santa Ana were gateway neighborhoods, where new immigrants often spent their first years settling into life in the United States. I had the opportunity to live on Townsend Street, a gateway neighborhood that was home mostly to Mexican immigrants and their children. *La Townsend*, as the neighborhood was known, was composed of rows of apartment buildings that spanned a couple of city blocks. Most apartment buildings were configured into courtyards, wherein two buildings faced each other, and socializing took place in the courtyards between. The apartment buildings were originally built as single-family units of either one or two bedrooms. Most units now housed multiple families and/or subleased space to other renters, some who were members of the extended family and others who were not. In the late 1990s, many of these immigrant neighbors worked in agricultural labor in the southern parts of the county. Others worked in the service industry, cleaning homes, offices, and other businesses.

In my hopeful Pentecostal spirit, I came to Santa Ana thinking I would help transform the community; instead, the community transformed me. As I got to know the people in the neighborhood, I came to understand that community could be more than an abstract theory. Community is about people looking out for each other; it is about being good neighbors. The neighbors I got to know on Townsend Street largely looked out for each other. One of my first days living in the community, I recall sitting in the living room of a local family from the neighborhood—second-generation, bilingual Mexican Americans who partnered with and received funding to assist with some of the organization's programming. The young couple, a husband-and-wife team, was talking to us about life in the community. The young woman at the time was preparing some breakfast burritos for the family at the kitchen stove. As she cooked and spoke to us, a young man from the neighborhood walked by the window of the apartment. She called out to him, "Do you want a burrito?" He nodded affirmatively. He had hardly finished nodding before she reached out the open window, holding out a burrito to him. I often saw acts of this type in the community and sometimes benefited from them.

I quickly learned that Townsend Street was home to the Townsend Street Gang. The initials CTR, which stood for Calle Townsend Rifa, were spray-painted along the alleyway to mark the gang's turf. Members of the gang convened on neighborhood sidewalks, in some cases relaxing and listening to music, in other cases dealing dope, and in other cases keeping watch over the neighborhood. Sometimes they did all of these at the same time. Rival neighborhoods were not far away, which meant conflict and confrontation were a part of life for many of the young gang members and even nongang members who were marked as being part of a particular neighborhood. I had grown up in a working-class neighborhood, knew of the local gangs in my area, and even knew a few gang affiliates, but I had never lived in a neighborhood where most young people, especially young men, experienced constant pressure to join a gang. On Townsend Street, the pressure was ever present, not merely because gang members were cool but also because gangs provided camaraderie and a means to survival. Ironically, the name the gang claimed, the street's namesake, likely had ties to the family of Cameron Townsend, a famous missionary who founded the Wycliffe Bible Translators and the Summer Institute of Linguistics. Townsend had grown up in Santa Ana and had family who held political office in the city.

While I did not promote the activities that the neighborhood gang was involved in, I came to recognize how the gang offered a community support system to young people. There was a reason the gang life was such a powerful draw: a sense of purpose. It also provided for many of the material needs of these young people, particularly for those who got involved with the drug-dealing business that the gang controlled locally. What I was most fascinated by, though, was the way that young people often felt compelled toward gang life. It was a type of calling that came to them in their community. As a calling, it often involved high risks and, for some young people whom I got to know, eventually led to death. I wondered how this calling could be re-envisioned as these young people were giving their lives up for a barrio.

These were young people whose families had largely been caught in the economic engine gears of transnational trade, often dispossessed in their homeland communities and now resettled in places that found uses for their labors but cared little for their lifeworlds. Adults in these neighborhoods worked multiple jobs and did what they could to provide for their families but had little time for recreation with their children. And these communities were highly surveilled, both in terms of local law enforcement and migratory laws. Once young people were labeled as gang-affiliated, they established an antagonistic relationship with local law enforcement. The lives of these young people and the purpose offered by the gangs were inextricable from these larger realities. The global, societal, and household realities of the community converged within the life opportunities of these young people. To be called by the barrio was a counterbalance to the dislocation that many young people had already experienced.

Through the organizational programming, we got to know many of the neighborhood families. Parents, often mothers, shared their needs and concerns with us about their children. We held space for them, and they often made space for us. Yet the experience was different for me than for someone coming in from a completely foreign context. I saw myself in the people of the neighborhood. I wondered about how the timing of my parents' migration, their region of origin, and my own social location provided me with a different experience from that of these other Mexican American children and young people I met in the neighborhood. These were my people. Mi pueblo. Mi gente. By chance, I grew up in a different type of neighborhood.

For the most part, the people received me as their own. I was given nicknames by the neighborhood kids and teens, a sign of acceptance in the community. Kids would say things like, "You look like my brother." I was invited over to visit people in their homes. I began as an outsider, but the community welcomed me.

My childhood memories of visiting Santa Ana became more vivid as I moved through the city. I later learned that some of my close family had lived in Santa Ana when they first migrated to Orange County. The very neighborhoods I was working in had welcomed some of my family decades before. I experienced it again. Un llamado. The barrio was calling me. I sensed the Spirit working in the barrio. My experience that summer was structured programmatically, but the community was calling me in a different way, in a way that was not solely linked to programs. I was being called home.

I continued on in my college education at Biola University and found ways to volunteer at the organization that housed the Kidworks program. Eventually, Kidworks spun off as its own nonprofit and evolved into a community development corporation, remembering its faith-based roots but also working through broader Christian-based and other grassroots partnerships. I maintained a relationship with Kidworks for years to come, and my soul maintains a relationship with the city of Santa Ana to this day. I eventually settled there and made it my home for over a dozen years. The community was wealthy in many ways, and I was especially drawn to its cultural wealth[3] and spiritual wealth.

One of the primary lessons I learned in the community was listening to the Spirit in the barrio. I recall one day that I was in a rush to arrive at one of the Kidworks learning centers to run a youth activity. I was a seminary student and commuted through Los Angeles and Orange County traffic. I had a difficult day earlier and was tired but was committed to my work with teens. In my mind, negative thoughts swirled that day: *Why are you doing this? You're wasting your time. No one is even going to come today.* I was convinced I was spinning my wheels that evening as I drove into the neighborhood. I walked up to the apartment complex that housed the learning center, thinking to myself, *I knew it! No one is going to come.* As if in response to my inner voice, I heard the voice of a child speak the words, "Ya llegue"

["I'm here / I've arrived"]. I looked down as a little girl, three or four years old, rode by on a tricycle and, in perfect timing, spoke to my inner voice: "Ya llegue." Some young people did show up that evening. And I needed to hear that still small voice beforehand. "Ya llegue." The Spirit was present. And just as on that evening, so often, the Spirit was present in the places and moments of the borderlands barrios.

CALLED TO COMMUNITY

My calling was not to save a community but to encounter the moving of the Spirit that was present in the community that had called me. Likewise, my focus on finding purpose through class mobility had been disrupted through my time at Kidworks. I would later learn that having a sustainable life was important, but for the time being, I recognized I was satisfied with being called *to* and *by* community.[4] The Spirit had moved through the people I encountered, and I had moved into another type of borderlands space. In her work on upwardly mobile Latines, Jody Agius Vallejo[5] highlights how many second-generation Latines seek and find ways to give back to the community. Santa Ana was one of the communities she identified as a space that many would give back to once they had moved away from the neighborhoods they had grown up in.

For me, calling was a type of returning back to roots I had not known about. I experienced a new sense of mobility—a mobility that called me in to be with my people.[6] Rather than being called to individual social mobility, the Spirit in the barrio called me to more deeply think about and engage the issues that blocked the sustainability of the lives of my neighbors. Being called to community also led to thinking about what it meant to sustain community. I was called back to the barrio, and the barrio has yet to leave me, even years later after I have moved to far-distant places. My views of callings have changed. They have expanded beyond the idea that one is called only to work in a formal ministry or religious setting. And yet, for me, calling has remained an invitation to cross back into my community and to restore and retain roots that were once severed.

CHAPTER NINE

Coyotaje as Care

I had heard the term *coyote* in stories told by close family friends, particularly from church friends, about their experiences crossing the border into the United States. These stories indicated that *coyotes* were people who assisted migrants in the act of physically crossing the border, guiding migrants across treacherous terrains to get to the United States, smuggling people through ports of entry, or providing access to other clandestine pathways of crossing over. In a course on migration during my PhD work, I was introduced to a more expansive related term—*coyotaje*. Coyotaje refers to strategies and practices that assist migrants in border-crossing and often include bureaucratic, labor, and livelihood considerations; these efforts might involve authorized or unauthorized means. In learning about this concept, I came to the realization that my maternal grandfather, Candelario, was involved in coyotaje.

Coyotaje encompasses a bundle of activities related to migration. After years of interacting with coyotes, David Spener[1] conceptualizes coyotaje as a sphere of activities that stand in resistance to systems of global apartheid rooted in exploitative relationships. Though coyotaje is most typically associated with someone who assists migrants to cross the border, the process of moving across hypersurveilled spaces entails more than physical movement through geographic terrain. The full scope of coyotaje may involve connecting migrants to resources, situating migrants within support networks, assisting migrants in finding means of self-support, and so on. Bureaucratic evasion and labor brokerage, for example, are often roles that coyotes engage in. That is, coyotaje may involve knowing one's way around papers and documents alongside moving across guarded territories. Furthermore, many of the activities of coyotaje are not illicit in nature, even if they are acts of resistance. Some forms of bureaucratic maneuvering, for example, may involve operating within the law while drawing on strategic relationships. At its essence, coyotaje is an act of helping people find a way where there appears to be none and building a life in a terrain that appears hostile to life. Through my circulations in Borderlands Pentecostalism, I saw the essence of coyotaje in multiple expressions, and often, the Spirit *en la frontera* was at work through these acts.

My grandfather's work with migrants and migration dealt with bureaucratic matters while he lived in Mexico. I grew up hearing stories about my grandfather working his connections with lawyers and government officials in order to help people get their *papeles*, including some relatives. My grandfather was known as an entrepreneur connected in the civic networks of the towns he called home. Much of his knowledge of bureaucratic proceedings began with a family notary public business in Tijuana. My grandfather lived in Tijuana for a season and then returned to Sonora with experience as a notary public; he leaned into his connections in civic and legal arenas and became adept at helping people obtain the required documents needed for legal migration. This often involved working through social networks and helping applicants fulfill bureaucratic requirements.

These acts of coyotaje point to a deeper essence—the work of helping people traverse barriers, often through newly forged and creative pathways. I draw on Spener's central premise in defining coyotaje:[2] it is an act of resistance to systems of global apartheid that are rooted in exploitative relationships. This is a coyotaje that seeks a workaround in a system that is profiting from the very people who are kept on the outside looking in. In other words, my primary focus is on a coyotaje that stands in resistance to oppressive and exploitative power relations and not merely a flouting of laws for personal profit or to exploit others. Despite the fact that some coyotes are predators, as education scholar Alma Zaragoza-Petty argues, for many migrants, "the trusted coyote from someone's community is still the safest bet." Expanding on this principal, Zaragoza-Petty advances the notion of the cultural coyote, "someone who travels between lands and carries others with them into new spaces."[3] In Borderlands Pentecostalism, the Spirit often operated through these border-crossing moves.

TRICKSTERS

The concept of coyotaje draws on long-standing traditions associated with trickster entities in mythology and lore. Such figures are present in a wide array of cultural folklore and within the Hebrew Scriptures. Figures such as Jacob, Tamar, and Abraham at times embody a trickster archetype as they employ cunning strategies to achieve their ends. To be clear, trickster figures reside along a spectrum of virtue, and some trickster figures prey on vulnerable populations. Some trickster archetypes are men who thrive on macho braggadocio and exploit women. Not all trickster figures are men, though, and not all are exploitative. Many tricksters are helpful, offering ingenious solutions to problems and embodying forms of resistance against more powerful entities. The coyote, the animal to which the concept of coyotaje is tied, has historically been known as a trickster. In a variety of Indigenous American cultures, the coyote appears in stories as a trickster.[4] Coyotes know how to bargain and get their way, and they may deceive or fool someone in the process.

Various scholars and writers attribute trickster-like characteristics to the Holy Spirit. For example, Zaida Maldonado Pérez describes the Holy Spirit as "the wild child of the Trinity, the Holy Subversive One."[5] Becca Whitla, citing the perspective of Rev. Susan Beaver of the Kanienkeha nation, notes that the term "wild child" may read problematically in some Indigenous American contexts. She does, however, offer a resonant corollary: "The Spirit changes to meet the needs of the contexts in which she is moving. She is a shape-shifting trickster who can be as Beaver describes her—healing Indigenous peoples and communities—or disturbing and disruptive where there is a need for confrontation and challenge against oppressive forces."[6]

In coyote figures, the human and the divine have converged partly because of this unpredictability. The work of Dan Flores,[7] who has written extensively about coyotes as a species, notes an interesting characteristic of theirs suggestive of humans' historical fascination with coyote figures. Coyotes are similar to humans in a variety of ways. They are highly adaptable animals. They have survived an array of ecological changes in their environments of origins. Also, like humans, they have migrated to disparate locales and have found new ways to adapt in places that were once completely unfamiliar to them. Flores posits that coyotes took on a special meaning for Indigenous peoples of the Paleolithic era because as humans witnessed changes in the flora and fauna of the Americas, they also witnessed the persistence of the coyote. Flores argues that the association between coyotes and humans does not originate with him but is a connection that Indigenous Americans made millennia ago.

While the great creatures of North America's bygone eras passed into extinction—the mastodon, the North American horse, the dire wolf, among others—coyotes found ways to persist. Humans saw themselves in this pattern of survival, perhaps aspirationally so. Furthermore, despite their adaptability, and unlike other species of canids, coyotes remained on the North American continent. They spread across a wide array of terrains, with unique incursions taking place in the last century, but they have historically been the paramount American species. Coyotes are both adaptable and grounded. Through this groundedness and adaptability, Flores believes they took on a deity-like status, primarily as a device to reveal to humans aspects of their own human nature.

In the borderlands region where my father's family hails from, the coyote remained a prominent trope, often used to describe someone who was astute and might use their wisdom for trickery. My father would often use phrases like "watch out, that guy's a real coyote," as a word of caution about someone who might try to swindle or take advantage of us. Yet to be a coyote was also celebrated. Sometimes my father or his brothers celebrated someone for being a coyote and completing a task where the challenges seemed insurmountable. That, too, was a coyote move. This connection came through prominently in an interaction I had with my paternal grandfather, Fermin Calvillo. When he first saw my high school football team pictures, he immediately noticed the coyote mascot and the coyote name emblazoned on the image. "Ahhh! Escogieron bien! Coyotes." ["Ahhh! They chose well! Coyotes"]. Coyotes might be sneaky, but they often win. The coyote is embedded into the cultural memory of my people. While it carries with it some negative connotations, opportunities to harness the life-giving characteristics of coyotes remain.

COYOTAJE IN THE HEBREW SCRIPTURES

Aspects of coyotaje resonate with the Exodus account in the Hebrew Scriptures. Representations of legality, labor, and livelihood show up in the liberation narrative featuring Moses, Miriam, and their mother, Jochebed, for example. Escalating already oppressive conditions, Pharaoh declared a widespread infanticide on the Hebrew people in which every son born to the Hebrews was to be thrown into the Nile (Ex. 1:22). Pharaoh was threatened by the growth and prosperity of the Hebrew population in Egypt. The current Pharaoh had forgotten the contributions of Joseph, who had helped Egypt prosper generations back. Instead, he enslaved the Hebrew people, appointing slave masters over them. The Hebrews built monumental structures in the Egyptian cities but were still dehumanized. Pharaoh wanted the benefits of the Hebrew labor force but did not want the Hebrews to prosper, fearing they would overthrow the Egyptians someday. Soon Pharaoh ordered the Hebrew midwives, who delivered the Hebrew infants, to kill all Hebrew boys being born. The Hebrew midwives eschewed his command because of their reverence for God. The Hebrews continued to grow. Pharaoh's ire escalated further as he commanded that all the Egyptians partake of the infanticide.

In these circumstances, a Levite family protected a young infant, Moses. Moses's mother, after his first three months of life, when she could hide him no longer, devised a plan to preserve the child's life, ironically, in the Nile River, the very river Pharaoh had commanded the Egyptians to hurl Hebrew infant boys into. Moses's mother built a papyrus basket coated with tar and pitch, which could float down the river while holding an infant within. Building the basket was an act of coyotaje, an act of finding and creating a way where no way seemed to be. An act of preserving life when death was imminent.

Moses was set into the Nile River in a basket, essentially as an unaccompanied minor. Certainly, no adult would accompany him. From a distance, though, his sister watched him as he floated along. Miriam now took on the role of coyote. She ensured that the child floated along safely. In some ways, she fulfilled the most traditional role of the coyote, ensuring that a migrant moving across borderlands reaches a place of safety and continues to live. Just as the Rio Grande serves as an important marker of the US-Mexico border, so, too, did Moses transition into a distinct social world through traversing a river. Moses was able to cross over with the help of his sister. As Miriam watched the basket float along, she observed as the infant and basket were discovered by none other than the daughter of Pharaoh. Pharaoh's daughter was on her way to bathe in the banks of the Nile River when she encountered the basket. The crying infant inside surprised her, and she was moved with compassion toward the child. She recognized that the infant was a Hebrew baby.

Here, Miriam's role as coyote makes a shift. She emerged from her place of observation and spoke to Pharaoh's daughter and her attendants as they had just found the baby. Miriam offered to bring a Hebrew woman to nurse the crying infant. I imagine that the baby's cries escalated the situation. The baby needed nourishment and soothing. This act of brokering, of offering to bring a Hebrew woman to nurse the baby, was an act of coyotaje. Miriam strategically returned with Moses's mother, who would then be able to nurse her own child. When Miriam brought her mother to Pharaoh's daughter, Pharaoh's daughter offered to pay the Hebrew mother to nurse the child. Miriam had not only brokered the nursing of her infant brother but also brokered a job for her mother. Here, Moses was given his name, which signified that Pharaoh's daughter had drawn him out of the waters.

Miriam enacted various tasks associated with coyotaje: watching over Moses, ensuring his safe arrival, communicating with someone in power to ensure his needs were met, and brokering a job for her mother. Likewise, as Karen Gonzalez[8] points out, the liberation of the Hebrew people begins with the acts of women: the midwives who flouted Pharaoh's commands; Jochabed, the Levite mother who preserved her son; and her daughter, Miriam, who guided her brother to safety. Yet Miriam's role goes beyond the preservation of Moses. The Scriptures identify her as a prophetess[9] and a leader,[10] alongside Aaron and Moses, who helped liberate the Hebrew people.[11] According-ing to Renita Weems, "Miriam is one of the few women in the Old Testament whom we come to know for herself—both for her strength and her weaknesses—and not solely for her role as some boy's mother or some man's wife." Miriam's acts of coyotaje culminate in a display of her creative gifts as she leads women in song and dance after the Hebrews cross the Red Sea.

BRINGING OTHERS ALONG

The coyotaje I envision is at its essence an act of community-building, an act of preserving life and of enacting liberation so as to ultimately build community together. This practice is a principle I admired about my paternal grandmother, Adelina Calvillo. One of the things my grandmother was great at doing was bringing people along with her wherever she went. With descendants numbering beyond one hundred individuals, when great-great-grandchildren are included in the count, she was often surrounded by people. I often marveled at my grandmother's patience with so many of her descendants. How did she not get tired of having so many people around her? She would often have children in her lap, infants in her arms, or someone lean-ing onto her shoulder. Her infectious smile rarely seemed to wane, and she was known to let out a chuckle as she would share a story or a memory with those around her.

With such a large family and having a living arrangement where family was always present, there was a particular detail that I marveled at about my grandmother: she somehow managed to draw other people in, from beyond the family circle, and welcomed them into the family. She made it a point to broaden her circle and bring others with her. More often than not, there were other women who accompanied her. Some of these women were there to help her and to give her support. And yet it was difficult to discern who was there to support whom. The support that was rendered was mutual, I came to conclude.

Ama, as she was known to us, found ways to build ties of kinship with others, as if she did not have enough kin already. This was not to the detriment of her existing kin. She knew our names and would often remind us that she was praying for us. When I traveled to distant shores or when my family relocated to the East Coast, I knew I could count on her prayers. And yet she managed to make space for others. The women Ama surrounded herself with were often immigrants. Ama was an immigrant herself, but she had migrated to the United States decades before. She was also a fronteriza who grew up not far from the US-Mexico border. Some of the women she communed with were more recent arrivals to the United States. Through their connection to Ama, these women had a place at the family table. They were welcomed at family gatherings and were part of the spiritual life of the family.

This act of bringing others along that I saw in my Ama I also saw in another mentor of mine, Dr. Jesse Miranda. Dr. Miranda was known in many circles as a bridge builder. He was a pioneer of religious education in Pentecostal circles and was ahead of his time in thinking through issues of intergenerational collaboration and of what it meant for older generations to empower younger generations. I had the honor of working with him for three years in a position at Vanguard University, which was housed in a center that Dr. Miranda founded. What began as the Center for Urban Studies and Hispanic Leadership was later renamed the Jesse Miranda Center for Hispanic Leadership. Dr. Miranda passed away in July 2019. Many voices emerged lamenting his transition but also expressing gratitude at his care and labor as a mentor and model in his field and in the church world.

I had the honor of seeing Dr. Miranda days before he passed away. The last time I saw him, his words were few. He and his family were preparing for their goodbyes. In that moment, at his home, with a handful of people around, he made a statement that will stay with me: "Do what God has called you to do and bring others with you." That was it. Those were the words Dr. Miranda left with me and with a couple of others who were present. It was a reminder of calling. A reminder to stay true to what I had to do. Yet his words were made all the more powerful by the second portion of his statement: "bring others with you." These two things—pursuing a divine calling and bringing others along—can never be separated. Dr. Miranda's words reminded me that calling is a communal act. To follow the divine call is to make space for others. The call cannot fully be lived out without bringing others with us.

COYOTAJE AND COMMUNITY

The essence of coyotaje operates beyond transactional exchanges when activated in a context of communal reciprocity. When we first moved to Boston in 2016, my partner, Nani, was pregnant with our son, Jonathan, and our sense of place and community was reconfigured. My parents came to visit us in Boston for our son's birth. During my parents' visit, my father, who likes to be aware of his surroundings, made it a point to start exploring our neighborhood. He borrowed my bicycle and began to ride around the area, getting to know the lay of the land. On the borderlands of the South End, adjacent to a different neighborhood, South Boston, my father found a path where he could ride alongside a river bed and a new urban park.

As my father rode the path he had discovered, he decided to stop and snap a picture of the scenery with his phone camera. Nearby, he spotted a man who appeared to be resting close to the path. He called out to the man to ask him to take a picture. My father struck up a conversation with him, learning about his background. This man,

Miguel,[12] was from Mexico. That detail was a surprise because he did not often encounter Mexicans in Boston, or at least not nearly as often as he did in California. As it turned out, Miguel had previously lived in the same region of Mexico that my father was from. He had also lived in Texas for a period, as had my father. Miguel lived at a local shelter. Daily he visited various places around the neighborhood and nightly returned to the shelter. He was an undocumented migrant, so his employment opportunities were limited, but he found seasonal work and was making do in Boston.

Miguel later confessed that he appreciated my father for asking him to serve as photographer that day. "No one asks me for anything," he said. When my father asked him to take a picture of him, he felt a sense of dignity and respect in that. In the weeks that followed, my father and Miguel became friends. Miguel showed my father around the neighborhood. He gave him different tips on where to eat and even where to access resources that he might need to get through the winter. "I know where they are giving away winter coats," he told my father as the frigid temperatures arrived. My father did not take up the offer but appreciated Miguel's local knowledge. In a gentrifying neighborhood like the South End, Miguel's knowledge of the neighborhood provided unique ways to experience the city.

On our first Thanksgiving in Boston, my father decided to get a haircut. He told us that Miguel had referred him to a barber, and we assumed this meant going to a barbershop. When my father returned with his hair newly cut, he had a story for us. The barber Miguel referred him to was a Puerto Rican man who lived at the shelter where Miguel lived. He used battery-operated clippers to give haircuts and sometimes set up shop near the path where my father rode his bicycle. Partway through my father's haircut, a pair of police officers patrolling the area rode by on bicycles and spotted the barber in action. The officers locked eyes with the barber and my father. Everyone froze. My father wondered if the officers were going to ticket them, yell at them, or perhaps do something worse. For a brief instance, the cold November air was thick with tension. Then a smile cracked through one of the officer's faces. The others warmed up as well. The first officer exclaimed, "I've seen it all!" My father and the barber reluctantly smiled. Soon, everyone laughed. The officers snapped a picture of the makeshift barbershop. When my father told us the story, we laughed as well. My mother shook her head in disbelief.

Miguel had created space for my father in the ways he could. He had shown my father hospitality and had shared his knowledge with him. My father also sought ways to create space for Miguel. Weeks earlier, after hearing the 2016 election results, Miguel sought an intervention. When news of Trump's victory emerged, Miguel expressed fear to my father. As an undocumented Mexican migrant, he began to expect the worst. He wondered if his life in the United States would be further threatened. After Miguel shared his fears, my father invited him to a church he had visited several times during his visit. The church, Leon de Juda, a bilingual Latine congregation, served immigrants and partnered with other immigrant-serving organizations. Miguel agreed to go with my father to a Sunday service.

That Sunday, the mayor of Boston made a guest appearance at Leon de Juda. The mayor, Marty Walsh, shared about his own life. He told parishioners that as the son of immigrants, he cared about immigrants. He told them he would do anything in his power to make immigrants feel safe. Elsewhere, Mayor Walsh went so far as to offer his own office as a sanctuary for immigrants. The fear started to wash away for Miguel, as he later told my father. He said that the words spoken at church that morning were directly for him. Toward the end of the service, my father sought someone from the church to pray with Miguel, who desired prayer. Several leaders came and prayed for him. One of them, a committed leader in mobilizing churches for migrant advocacy, Daniel Montañez, would later become one of my students at Boston University. Miguel walked away in much better spirits that day and expressed a sense of peace that he had not felt in a long time.

The following year, Miguel would join my family and me for Thanksgiving after we had moved to another neighborhood in Boston. He and my father remained in communication via cell phone for several years after. We eventually lost touch with Miguel, but during that season, we shared space with him. Miguel brought my father along in the neighborhood, allowing him to become acquainted with a completely new setting. My father affirmed Miguel's story and facilitated his engagement with spaces previously unfamiliar to him. This essence of coyotaje was present for only a season of accompaniment, and I remain grateful for Miguel's presence in this season.

COYOTAJE AND FAITH

The faith communities I moved in made room for expanding visions of coyotaje, even if they did not realize it. Forms of coyotaje have often been conceived of as services procured from someone with resources by someone who is in need of that individual's knowledge or services. However, I also recognized in my upbringing examples of coyotaje as ongoing expressions of mutuality, with aims of opening pathways toward thriving and sustainability in the face of systems of inequality and injustice. As I observed the Spirit *en las fronteras*, forms of coyotaje often manifested in systems of care and support that the faithful provided for each other. In the borderlands, among people living on the margins, coyotaje was often the way to get through and make it in life. Coyotaje might have looked like a place to stay, a job opportunity, a plate of food, life-giving information, or a caring prayer. These practices of coyotaje moved through our communities and often sustained them; they generated visions of other and unknown pathways where the options and resources seemed exhausted. They were acts of making and finding ways with and for others.

Conclusion

In Remembrance

For years, I have commemorated a forgotten memory, a blank space in my personal story. I awoke disoriented, leaning against my car, a stranger asking if he should call an ambulance for me. I began to piece together what had ensued, replaying the sequence of events in my mind. I had parked my vehicle in a parking lot in Westminster, California, where I planned to enter a convenience store and use the ATM inside. A different stranger approached me as I got out of my car and asked me for something in muffled words. I told him I was sorry that I could not give him anything, not realizing I misunderstood what he had asked for. In a calm and quiet manner, he had actually uttered, "Let me see your Honda keys." As I regained consciousness, the man's words lingered in my memory, and I realized I had survived an attempted carjacking.

That day, I awakened to a new reality. My memory of this life-defying confrontation was a mental gap never to be filled. In the days and months to come, my capacity to remember was diminished. I still held long-term memories from years back but struggled to remember details from recent interactions. The incident happened the week after one of the most intellectually rigorous experiences of my academic career: I had defended my dissertation proposal for my PhD program in sociology at the University of California at Irvine. The prior weeks, I had studied and mentally organized hundreds of pages' worth of material. After the incident, I struggled to retain information from a few pages of reading. This was my new normal: coming to grips with my memory limitations.

As I went through the recovery process, my kin came through for me. My parents, in-laws, and extended family checked in on me frequently. My life partner, Puanani, walked alongside me through the process of healing, showing patience as I attempted to return to my previous self. At the time, I was serving in a pastoral role at El Puente Community Church, a small bilingual community-based church that worked collaboratively with local residents and organizations. In the days following the attack, members of my church showed up at my home and sat with me. Many of these folks had experienced violence in their own lives. Some had lost loved ones to gang violence. Some had seen violence in their homelands or in the process of migration. Some had survived abusive relationships. They took the time to sit with me. They did not ask many questions. They sat. And in those moments of co-presence, of spiritual communion, the Spirit soothed my soul.

The grace shown to me by these kinfolk provided a special kind of healing, one that perhaps defied the type of healing I was hoping and praying for. From my Pentecostal healing perspective, I wanted to experience a complete and rapid healing. If not an immediate supernatural healing, I hoped to experience a swift recovery. After all, awakening from the attack was a type of resurrection for me.[1] I was given a new chance at life. To be alive was to experience the power of Jesus Christ's resurrection. It was only fitting that in experiencing God's protection and resurrection power, I would return to my "normal" self. The momentum of new life and the support of kin kept me pressing forward in a positive attitude despite not getting the type of healing I thought I wanted.

The reality that unfolded proved to be different than what I hoped and prayed for. My recovery did not unfold in a swift, linear fashion. Rather, my inconsistencies with memory continued. This was a new type of borderlands for me. As with many borderlands, it represented a multi-positional experience. On the one hand, I had crossed over from the threat of death to life. My memories would be marked by the before and after of this experience.[2] The traversing, the crossing over, the rupture between past and present were a reality that many of my immigrant neighbors experienced. In having survived, I was grateful for life. On the other hand, I was not who I used to be—and never would be. I was in a state of liminality, a state of "not-yet." I was not fully healed.

I was reminded of the "already but not yet" theology of the kingdom of God[3] that I had learned about in seminary, a theology that resonated with my Pentecostal background. This theology spoke to the eschatological foretaste reflected in the communion practices I knew. As Pentecostal theologian Simon Chan[4] sums it up, "This actualization takes place in the Eucharist, where the 'already' and the 'not yet' are held together." Likewise, this theology within a broader evangelical context provided space for my Pentecostal imagination to continue thinking about how the gifts of the Spirit active today pointed to the eschaton.

And yet what I most wanted was the already, but I felt stuck in the not-yet. This was not the not-yet of the five-year plans and vision statements I had learned about in evangelicalism. Neither was it the not-yet of prophetic words I had heard from gifted preachers in Pentecostal contexts. While these could be helpful tools, their mastery could also be wielded as commodifications of the future.[5] Instead, in this state of in-betweenness, this state of waiting, I began learning to embrace a more permanent borderlands reality, "breathing room in the pause of the not-yet."[6] Lived Pentecostal theologies allowed for this state of not-yet. I was reminded of the yearnings I learned to express at the altar, petitions that sometimes persisted across years and were often answered in ways unexpected. I was also reminded of the ongoing nature of testimonios, adding to the story over time, even if at given moments stories were presented as fully complete. Our borderlands circulations, after all, were ongoing, generational even. We were a "border people."[7]

HEALING

An unexpected source of healing came as I was finally able to re-engage in my doctoral dissertation process. I went out into the field as an ethnographer and studied how faith shaped the ethnic identity of Mexican immigrants. In my project, I compared the experiences of Catholics and evangelicals in Santa Ana, the city where I lived. The project involved interviewing people about their migration experiences, their sense of building ethnic community in the United States, and how their faith narratives intersected with their migration narratives. Along with interviews, I spent time with collaborators within their own faith communities. I asked them to share their spiritual worlds with me, to the extent that they felt comfortable, and got to know the spaces they called home.

Hearing the testimonios of these saints was healing. They were making homes in the borderlands of the here-and-not-yet. There was wisdom in their testimonios. I heard stories of adaptation, stories of hardship, stories of tragedy, and stories of overcoming. People opened their homes to me and shared aspects of their lives with trust and vulnerability. These friends, neighbors, and near kin invited me to the table and shared family recipes. Some who were undocumented lived in a constant state of liminality; there was an underlying caution that permeated their lives, but they also established deep networks of trust where they could experience joy and celebrate in community. Others told tales of racialized liminality alongside their migration status. They faced worksite discrimination, encountered residential inequalities, and avoided ongoing community surveillance from law enforcement. The experience of women, often on the margins of formal church leadership positions, shone through for their leadership in the community. It was often women who led in the neighborhood processions or prayer gatherings, whose networks provided a safety net for those in need and whose creative talents beautified the world around them. These immigrants who were often talked about as powerless, and faced real structural barriers toward societal integration, exercised agency. They built community in these legal, geographic, and social borderlands.

As I visited the churches of my research collaborators, other forms of healing occurred in me. While my recollection abilities did not instantly improve, my body responded to particular experiences in ways that hearkened back to deeply held memories. When I visited immigrant Pentecostal churches, I immediately remembered in embodied ways the practices of my family. I could immediately feel the ways my parents' generation, and their parents' generation, worshipped in the borderlands. My younger self also worshipped in these spaces. The Spirit moved through the *coritos*. "Donde esta el espiritu de Dios," one *corito* rang out ["Where the Spirit of God is"]. The vibrations of the guitars, drums, and bass shook me as the words of the song came through. "Hay libertad, hay libertad," it refrained ["There is liberty, there is liberty"]. I had adapted to meet the needs of a diverse audience at my church and to work with a diverse coalition of churches. Yet these Borderlands Pentecostal experiences felt right to my soul as I spent time in these faith communities, received as a member of the family returning home.

I also visited the Catholic communities of some research collaborators. For some time, I had internalized a sense of being different from my Catholic co-ethnics. As a Pentecostal, I was in the religious minority. Yet with the way my Catholic neighbors embodied the grace of the sacraments with care in the neighborhood, I found healing there too. As my Catholic neighbors sacralized the spaces deemed profane, covering the streets in prayer and in reverence through processions and feast days, I began to encounter an aspect of the body of Christ and the barrio of Christ that I had not fully embraced before. Spiritual community can be ritualized in physical, tangible places where we live; it need not be confined to cathedrals and temples. These Catholic collaborators welcomed me into their communities.

Through these moments of following my research collaborators in the field, I began to sense the Spirit moving throughout the barrios and blocks of Santa Ana. The wind blows where it wishes,[8] and I found myself following the Spirit that was moving through the Santa Ana borderlands. The Spirit was mysterious and unknown, taking me to places and expressions I had not known before, alongside spaces that became immediately familiar and easy to follow along with. The mystery of the Spirit became normal in these borderlands. While on one level I was writing as a sociologist, documenting my observations as meticulously as possible, unconsciously I was experiencing the healing of the Spirit that my peoples knowingly and unknowingly offered to me.

With the support of a team made up largely of my spouse, my parents, and my children, along with the encouragement of many friends, I completed and defended my dissertation in the spring of 2016. Prior to that, I made the difficult decision of stepping away from my lead role as pastor of El Puente Community Church. The duties of that role alongside my studies stretched me beyond capacity. I retained my connection to that community but could not continue fulfilling the same duties amid my recovery process and during my research. At the time, I was in denial about being in recovery, but my body reminded me. As I neared graduation with a PhD in sociology, I received an offer of a dream job at Boston University School of Theology. My completion of that degree and of obtaining that job was truly a community effort. That PhD belongs to my family and my Santa Ana community. The Spirit they imparted on me, the anointing to finish those tasks, kept me alive.

EL ESPIRITU IN THE BORDERLANDS

When thinking of the experiences of Borderlands Pentecostals, I wonder about what we are allowed to remember and what we leave behind. I have journeyed through the modes of belonging that I and others in my community have drawn on to make a way while following the Spirit in and through the borderlands. The resonances that we encounter in the borderlands remain as reminders of who we are, who our ancestors are, and how the Spirit has continually been at work, forging a way toward life where perhaps a way is not seen. My hope is that in reading this, resonances of the Spirit have moved in readers, that aspects of readers' self, once forgotten or set aside but essential to their well-being, may stir up in them and contribute to their wholeness. My hope is that in this tapestry of stories, the Spirit has resonated in you.

I close this book with a final image: I am reminded of my visits back to my parents' family home, now with a family of my own. During mealtime there, my children frequently run outside to pick lemons so as to squeeze lemon juice onto their favorite *fideo* soup—*sopita*, as they call it. They pick lemons from the tree that my nana Josefina planted, the engrafted tree. The tree reminds me of Nana Josefina and of how she cultivated the engrafted citrus tree. While she never got to meet my children, her gardening knowledge continues to bless my children through a tree that embodies our borderlands journey—bitter in places, sweet in others, and still branching out and in as it is tended to by familia. As the tree rustles in the wind, I am reminded that it will not be here forever, but the fruits that fall have the potential for sprouting seedlings anew.

Notes

INTRODUCTION

1 Fullerton Tokers Town.
2 Ada María Isasi-Díaz, *La Lucha Continues: Mujerista Theology* (Maryknoll, NY: Orbis Books, 1996).
3 Alejandro Nava, *Street Scriptures: Between God and Hip-Hop* (Chicago: University of Chicago Press, 2022), https://doi.org/10.7208/chicago/9780226819150.
4 Lloyd Daniel Barba, *Sowing the Sacred: Mexican Pentecostal Farmworkers in California* (New York: Oxford University Press, 2022); Thomas A. Tweed, *Crossing and Dwelling: A Theory of Religion* (Cambridge, MA: Harvard University Press, 2009).
5 David Carrasco, *Religions of Mesoamerica: Second Edition* (Long Grove, IL: Waveland Press, 2013).
6 Jacqueline M. Hidalgo, "'So Many of Our Destinies Are Tied beyond Our Understanding': Rethinking Religious Hybridity in Latinx/o/a Contexts," *Missiology* 50 (1): 17–26, https://doi.org/10.1177/00918296211041047.
7 Todd L. VanPool and Christine S. VanPool, "Visiting the Horned Serpent's Home: A Relational Analysis of Paquimé as a Pilgrimage Site in the North American Southwest," *Journal of Social Archaeology* 18, no. 3 (2018): 306–324, https://doi.org/10.1177/1469605318762819.
8 Paquime was abandoned prior to the arrival of European explorers, and scholars believe descendants of its original inhabitants remain in the region, though identifying a precise community of descent has been difficult. See Paul E. Minnus and Michael E. Whalen, *Ancient Paquimé and the Casas Grandes World* (Tucson: University of Arizona Press, 2015).
9 Kat Armas, *Abuelita Faith: What Women on the Margins Teach Us about Wisdom, Persistence, and Strength* (Grand Rapids, MI: Brazos Press, 2021).
10 Rudy V. Busto, *King Tiger: The Religious Vision of Reies López Tijerina* (Albuquerque: University of New Mexico Press, 2006), 97.
11 Native peoples especially received the brunt of colonial incursions.
12 Daisy L. Machado, "The Unnamed Woman: Justice, Feminists, and the Undocumented Woman," in *A Reader in Latina Feminist Theology*, ed.

María Pilar Aquino, Daisy L. Machado, and Jeanette Rodríguez (Austin: University of Texas Press), 161–176, https://doi.org/10.7560/705098-010.

13 Gloria Anzaldúa, *Borderlands* (San Francisco: Aunt Lute Books, 1999), 3.

14 Likewise, some move through borderlands with the privilege to establish policies and laws that favor them.

15 Anzaldúa, *Borderlands*.

16 Danièle Hervieu-Léger and John A. Farhat, "Religion as Memory: Reference to Tradition and the Constitution of a Heritage of Belief in Modern Societies," in *Religion: Beyond a Concept*, ed. Hent de Vries (New York: Fordham University, 2008), 245–258.

17 Keri Day, *Notes of a Native Daughter: Testifying in Theological Education* (Grand Rapids, MI: Wm. B. Eerdmans Publishing, 2021).

18 Gastón Espinosa, *Latino Pentecostals in America: Faith and Politics in Action* (Cambridge, MA: Harvard University Press, 2014); Daniel Ramírez, *Migrating Faith: Pentecostalism in the United States and Mexico in the Twentieth Century* (Chapel Hill: UNC Press Books, 2015).

19 Albert Camarillo, *Chicanos in California: A History of Mexican Americans in California* (San Francisco: Boyd & Fraser, 1984).

20 This rhythm lasted for roughly three years, but the revival extended until 1915. See Frank Bartleman, *Azusa Street* (Newberry, FL: Bridge Logos Foundation, 1980).

21 Estrelda Y. Alexander, *Black Fire: One Hundred Years of African American Pentecostalism* (Downers Grove, IL: InterVarsity Press, 2011); Gastón Espinosa, *William J. Seymour and the Origins of Global Pentecostalism: A Biography and Documentary History* (Durham, NC: Duke University Press, 2014).

22 I use the panethnic term "Latino" in reference to Latino Pentecostals as it is the term most typically used by members of the community. I use "Latine" in reference to general panethnic populations of Latin American and Hispanophone Caribbean diasporas.

23 Barba, *Sowing the Sacred*; David M. Gustafson, "Pentecostal Evangelist Cenna Osterberg and the Azusa Street Mission," *Pietsten*, 35, no. 2 (2020), http://www.pietisten.org/xxxv/2/cenna_osterberg.html.

24 Ramírez, *Migrating Faith*, 4; see also Bartleman, *Azusa Street*.

25 Ramírez, *Migrating Faith*, 4.

26 Arlene Sanchez-Walsh, *Latino Pentecostal Identity: Evangelical Faith, Self, and Society* (New York: Columbia University Press, 2003); Espinosa, *Latino Pentecostals in America*.

27 Espinosa, *Latino Pentecostals in America*. Cape Verdean pastor Adolph Rosa early on played an important role in reaching Spanish speakers, including Mexicans, and also merits attention. As a former Methodist pastor, his contact with the Azusa Street revival propelled him to preach the Pentecostal message in Oakland, California, to both Portuguese and Spanish speakers.

28 Clifton L. Holland, *The Religious Dimension in Hispanic Los Angeles: A Protestant Case Study* (Pasadena, CA: William Carey Library, 1974).

29 Emerson Little, "Recognizing the History behind the Bernal House," *Fullerton Observer*, June 11, 2020, https://fullertonobserver.com/2020/06/11/recognizing-the-history-behind-the-bernal-house/.

30 Tweed, *Crossing and Dwelling*.

31 See Barba, *Sowing the Sacred*, on the practices of scripturalizing that some Pentecostals engage in, reading their own testimonies in parallel with the acts of the apostles.

32 Barba, *Sowing the Sacred*; Ramirez, *Migrating Faith*; Mike Davis, "Planet of Slums," *New Left Review* 26 (2004): 5.

CHAPTER ONE

1 Tomas Jimenez, *Replenished Ethnicity: Mexican Americans, Immigration, and Identity* (Berkeley: University of California Press, 2010).

2 My mother's aunt and uncle had moved to Fullerton to pastor Templo El Buen Pastor church.

3 The church retains these characteristics as of this writing.

4 Gilda L. Ochoa, *Becoming Neighbors in a Mexican American Community: Power, Conflict, and Solidarity* (Austin: University of Texas Press, 2004).

5 A term denoting Mexican Americans who have limited connections to Mexican culture, often used pejoratively.

6 Truncated or limited.

7 Elizabeth E. Brusco, *The Reformation of Machismo: Evangelical Conversion and Gender in Colombia* (Austin: University of Texas Press, 2011).

8 This nickname for El Paso was often shortened to El Chuco.

9 The institute was founded by Alice Luce, an Episcopalian missionary from England who had worked in India and became a key Pentecostal figure among Latinos in the first half of the twentieth century. See Gaston Espinosa, *Latino Pentecostals in America: Faith and Politics in Action* (Cambridge, MA: Harvard University Press, 2014).

10 Daniel Ramírez, "Alabaré a Mi Señor: Culture and Ideology in Latino Protestant Hymnody," in *Los Evangelicos: Portraits of Latino Protestantism in the United States*, ed. Juan F. Martinez and Lindy Scott (Eugene, OR: Wipf and Stock Publishers, 2009), 149–170.

11 Edwin David Aponte, "Understanding Spirituality and Theologizing Popular Protestantism," in *The Wiley Blackwell Companion to Latinoax Theology*, ed. Orlando O. Espín (Wiley, 2023), 472–490, https://doi.org/10.1002/9781119870333.ch26.

12 "Tune: Alabaré," Hymnary, accessed February 27, 2024, https://hymnary.org/tune/alabare_alonso_pagan.

13 Robert Carlton Savage, ed., *Favoritos Juveniles: Los Himnos y Coritos Más Populares entre la Juventud Latinoamericana* (Grand Rapids, MI: Musica Singspiracion, 1973).

14 Antonio Eduardo Alonso, "Latinx Contributions to Liturgical and Sacramental Theology," in *The Wiley Blackwell Companion to Latinoax Theology*, ed. Orlando O. Espín (Wiley, 2023), 292–310, https://doi .org/10.1002/9781119870333.ch16.

15 Espinosa documents the importance of this hymnal, as compiled by Henry C. Ball. Espinosa, *Latino Pentecostals in America*.

16 Edwin David Aponte, *¡Santo! Varieties of Latino/a Spirituality* (Maryknoll, NY: Orbis Books, 2012).

17 Christopher L. Busey and Carolyn Silva, "Troubling the Essentialist Discourse of Brown in Education: The Anti-Black Sociopolitical and Sociohistorical Etymology of Latinxs as a Brown Monolith," *Educational Researcher* 50, no. 3 (October 2020): 176–186; Tatiana Flores, "'Latinidad Is Cancelled' Confronting an Anti-Black Construct," *Latin American and Latinx Visual Culture* 3, no. 3 (2021): 58–79; Juliet Hooker, "Hybrid Subjectivities, Latin American Mestizaje, and Latino Political Thought on Race," *Politics, Groups, and Identities* 2 (June 2014): 188–201.

18 Nadia Yamel Flores-Yeffal, *Migration-Trust Networks: Social Cohesion in Mexican US-Bound Emigration* (College Station: Texas A&M University Press, 2013), http://muse.jhu.edu/book/23152.

19 Aida I. Ramos, Gerardo Martí, and Mark T. Mulder, "The Strategic Practice of 'Fiesta' in a Latino Protestant Church: Religious Racialization and the Performance of Ethnic Identity," *Journal for the Scientific Study of Religion* 59, no. 1 (2020): 161–179.

20 Tom Miller, *Revenge of the Saguaro: Offbeat Travels through America's Southwest* (El Paso, TX: Cinco Puntos Press, 2010).

21 Deborah L. Berho, Gerardo Marti, and Mark T. Mulder, "Global Pentecostalism and Ethnic Identity Maintenance among Latino Immigrants: A Case Study of a Guatemalan Neo-Pentecostal Congregation in the Pacific Northwest," *Pneuma* 39, nos. 1–2 (2017): 5–33.

22 Tony Tian-Ren Lin, *Prosperity Gospel Latinos and Their American Dream* (Chapel Hill: UNC Press Books, 2020).

23 "We lost, Lord!"

24 "We have victory in Jesus Christ!"

CHAPTER TWO

1 Frank Bartleman, *Azusa Street* (Newberry, FL: Bridge Logos Foundation, 1980).

2 Lloyd Barba, "The Borderlands Aesthetics of Mexican American Pentecostalism," in *Protestant Aesthetics and the Arts*, ed. Sarah Covington and Kathryn Reklis (New York: Routledge, 2020).

3 Keri Day, *Notes of a Native Daughter: Testifying in Theological Education* (Grand Rapids, MI: Wm. B. Eerdmans Publishing, 2021).

4 Arlene Sanchez-Walsh, *Latino Pentecostal Identity: Evangelical Faith, Self, and Society* (New York: Columbia University Press, 2003).

5 Pablo Vila, *Border Identifications: Narratives of Religion, Gender, and Class on the U.S.-Mexico Border* (Austin: University of Texas Press, 2005).

6 See Brusco on how men's lives were often transformed through these conversion experiences. Elizabeth E. Brusco, *The Reformation of Machismo: Evangelical Conversion and Gender in Colombia* (Austin: University of Texas Press, 2011).

7 Radio and television host Pedro Ferriz Santa Cruz was key in disseminating ideas about UFOs to Mexican audiences starting in 1939.

CHAPTER THREE

1 Luis D. León, *La Llorona's Children: Religion, Life, and Death in the US–Mexican Borderlands* (Berkeley: University of California Press, 2004); Leah Payne, *Gender and Pentecostal Revivalism: Making a Female Ministry in the Early Twentieth Century* (New York: Springer, 2015).

2 Victor Turner, *The Ritual Process: Structure and Anti-Structure* (New York: Routledge, 1995).

3 Elaine Peña, *Performing Piety: Making Space Sacred with the Virgin of Guadalupe* (Berkeley: University of California Press, 2011).

4 See Vondey for discussion on the importance of the Pentecostal altar as theological metaphor. Wolfgang Vondey, *Pentecostal Theology: Living the Full Gospel* (London: Bloomsbury Publishing, 2017).

5 León, *La Llorona's Children*; Edward Flores, *God's Gangs: Barrio Ministry, Masculinity, and Gang Recovery* (New York: NYU Press, 2014).

6 A pseudonym.

7 T. M. Luhrmann, *When God Talks Back: Understanding the American Evangelical Relationship with God* (New York: Knopf Doubleday Publishing Group, 2012).

8 León, *La Llorona's Children*.

9 Gastón Espinosa, *Latino Pentecostals in America: Faith and Politics in Action* (Cambridge, MA: Harvard University Press, 2014).

10 Phil. 2:10–11.

CHAPTER FOUR

1 Ada María Isasi-Díaz, *La Lucha Continues: Mujerista Theology* (Maryknoll, NY: Orbis Books, 1996).

2 Bill Broyles et al., *Last Water on the Devil's Highway: A Cultural and Natural History of Tinajas Altas* (Tucson: University of Arizona Press, 2014).

3 Matthew 3:17.

4 Rachel Havrelock, *River Jordan: The Mythology of a Dividing Line* (Chicago: University of Chicago Press, 2011), 82.

5 Patrick B. Reyes, *Nobody Cries When We Die: God, Community, and Surviving to Adulthood* (St. Louis: Chalice Press, 2016).

6 Isasi-Díaz, *La Lucha Continues.*

7 Barbara Andrea Sostaita, "'Water, Not Walls:' Toward a Religious Study of Life That Defies Borders," *American Religion* 1, no. 2 (2019): 74–97.

8 Barbara Sostaita (2019) argues that such items are an extension of migrants' bodies. Sostaita, "'Water, Not Walls.'"

9 See Sostaita (2023) for a discussion on the power of touch at the borderlands. Barbara Sostaita, "Borrando La Frontera: Ana Teresa Fernández's Border Communion," in *The Routledge Handbook of Material Religion*, ed. Pooyan Tamimi Arab, Jennifer Scheper Hughes, and S. Brent Rodríguez-Plate (New York: Routledge, 2023), 360–370.

CHAPTER FIVE

1 Gerardo Martí, "Maranatha (O Lord, Come): The Power-Surrender Dynamic of Pentecostal Worship," *Liturgy* 33, no. 3 (2018): 20–28, https://doi.org/10.1080/0458063X.2018.1449515.

2 Keri Day, *Azusa Reimagined: A Radical Vision of Religious and Democratic Belonging* (Stanford, CT: Stanford University Press, 2022).

3 Amos Yong, *The Spirit Poured Out on All Flesh: Pentecostalism and the Possibility of Global Theology* (Grand Rapids, MI: Baker Academic, 2005).

4 Amos Yong, *Discerning the Spirit(s): A Pentecostal-Charismatic Contribution to Christian Theology of Religions* (Eugene, OR: Wipf and Stock Publishers, 2019).

5 Martí, "Maranatha."

6 Margaret Poloma and John Green, *The Assemblies of God : Godly Love and the Revitalization of American Pentecostalism* (New York: New York University Press, 2010).

7 Yong, *Discerning the Spirit(s).*

8 Elizabeth Conde-Frazier, "Dancing with the Wild Child," in *Latina Evangélicas: A Theological Survey from the Margins*, ed. Loida Martell-Otero, Zaida Maldonado Pérez, and Elizabeth Conde-Frazier (Eugene, OR: Wipf and Stock Publishers, 2013), 14–32.

9 Poloma and Green, *The Assemblies of God.*

10 Victor Turner, *The Ritual Process: Structure and Anti-Structure* (New York: Routledge, 1995), https://doi.org/10.4324/9781315134666.

11 Angela Tarango, *Choosing the Jesus Way: American Indian Pentecostals and the Fight for the Indigenous Principle* (Chapel Hill: UNC Press Books, 2014).

12 Elizabeth D. Ríos, "'The Ladies Are Warriors': Latina Pentecostalism and Faith-Based Activism in New York City," in *Latino Religions and Civic Activism in the United States*, ed. Gastón Espinosa, Virgilio P. Elizondo, and Jesse Miranda, (New York: Oxford University Press 2005), 197–214.

13 Leah Payne, *Gender and Pentecostal Revivalism: Making a Female Ministry in the Early Twentieth Century* (New York: Springer, 2015).

14 Women were also the majority of Sunday School teachers and leaders of other children ministries such as vacation Bible schools.

CHAPTER SIX

1 Amos Yong, *Who Is the Holy Spirit: A Walk with the Apostles* (Brewster, MA: Paraclete Press, 2011).

2 My church communities did practice anointing people with oil for unique moments of prayer and commissioning.

3 Erika D. Gault and Travis Harris, *Beyond Christian Hip Hop: A Move toward Christians and Hip Hop* (New York: Routledge, 2019).

4 Imani Perry, *Prophets of the Hood: Politics and Poetics in Hip Hop* (Durham, NC: Duke University Press, 2004).

5 Daniel White Hodge, *Hip Hop's Hostile Gospel: A Post-Soul Theological Exploration* (Boston, MA: Brill, 2016).

6 Anthony B. Pinn, *Noise and Spirit: The Religious and Spiritual Sensibilities of Rap Music* (New York: New York University Press, 2003), https://muse.jhu.edu/book/10706.

7 Murray Forman, *The 'Hood Comes First: Race, Space, and Place in Rap and Hip-Hop* (Middleton, CT: Wesleyan University Press, 2002).

8 Jerry Hicks, "Buena Park High Teaches Lesson in the 3 Rs: Resolve, Respect and Reconciliation," *Los Angeles Times*, May 7, 1998, sec. California, https://www.latimes.com/archives/la-xpm-1998-may-07-me-47199-story.html.

9 Some scholars note this pattern in Los Angeles area schools. Pierrette Hondagneu-Sotelo and Walter Thompson-Hernandez, "Being Brown, Knowing Black," in *South Central Dreams: Finding Home and Building Community in South LA*, ed. P. Hondagneu-Sotelo and M. Pastor (New York: New York University Press, 2021), 117–154.

10 Su'ad Abdul Khabeer, *Muslim Cool: Race, Religion, and Hip Hop in the United States* (New York: New York University Press, 2016).

11 Jon Ivan Gill, *Underground Rap as Religion: A Theopoetic Examination of a Process Aesthetic Religion* (New York: Routledge, 2019).

12 Raquel Z. Rivera, *New York Ricans from the Hip Hop Zone* (New York: Palgrave Macmillan, 2003).

13 Khabeer, *Muslim Cool*.

CHAPTER SEVEN

1 In 2007, Biola appointed as its president Dr. Barry Corey, who was ordained with the Assemblies of God. His appointment reflected the increasing openness to Pentecostalism in some sectors of Evangelicalism.

2 Arlene Sanchez-Walsh, *Latino Pentecostal Identity: Evangelical Faith, Self, and Society* (New York: Columbia University Press, 2003), 1.

3 Juan F. Martinez and Lindy Scott, *Los Evangelicos: Portraits of Latino Protestantism in the United States* (Eugene, OR: Wipf and Stock Publishers, 2009).

4 Sanchez-Walsh, *Latino Pentecostal Identity*.

5 Peter L. Berger, *The Sacred Canopy: Elements of a Sociological Theory of Religion* (Garden City, NY: Doubleday, 1967).

6 Robert Chao Romero, *Brown Church: Five Centuries of Latina/o Social Justice, Theology, and Identity* (Downers Grove, IL: InterVarsity Press, 2020).

7 Brad Christerson, Korie L. Edwards, and Michael Oluf Emerson, *Against All Odds: The Struggle for Racial Integration in Religious Organizations* (New York: New York University Press, 2005).

8 Michael O. Emerson and Christian Smith, *Divided by Faith: Evangelical Religion and the Problem of Race in America* (New York: Oxford University Press, 2000).

9 William Edward Burghardt DuBois, *The Souls of Black Folk* (New York: Blue Heron Press, 1904).

CHAPTER EIGHT

1 Richard N. Pitt, *Divine Callings: Understanding the Call to Ministry in Black Pentecostalism* (New York: New York University Press, 2012).

2 Larry Acosta, "Letting God Change You," presented at the 68th Annual Missions Conference, Biola University, April 16, 1997, https://digitalcommons.biola.edu/missions-conference/MC1997/mc1997sch/4.

3 Robert Chao Romero and Jeff Liou, *Christianity and Critical Race Theory: A Faithful and Constructive Conversation* (Grand Rapids, MI: Baker Academic, 2023).

4 Patrick B. Reyes, *Nobody Cries When We Die: God, Community, and Surviving to Adulthood* (St. Louis: Chalice Press, 2016).

5 Jody Agius Vallejo, *Barrios to Burbs: The Making of the Mexican-American Middle Class* (Stanford, CA: Stanford University Press, 2012).

6 Angela Tarango, *Choosing the Jesus Way: American Indian Pentecostals and the Fight for the Indigenous Principle* (Chapel Hill: UNC Press Books, 2014).

CHAPTER NINE

1 David Spener, *Clandestine Crossings: Migrants and Coyotes on the Texas-Mexico Border* (Ithaca, NY: Cornell University Press, 2011).

2 Spener, *Clandestine Crossings.*
3 Alma Zaragoza-Petty, *Chingona: Owning Your Inner Badass for Healing and Justice* (Minneapolis: Augsburg Fortress Publishers, 2022), 124
4 Patrick B. Reyes, *The Purpose Gap: Empowering Communities of Color to Find Meaning and Thrive* (Westminster, UK: John Knox Press, 2021).
5 Zaida Maldonado Pérez, "Dancing with the Wild Child," in *Latina Evangélicas: A Theological Survey from the Margins*, ed. Loida Martell-Otero, Zaida Maldonado Pérez, and Elizabeth Conde-Frazier (Eugene, OR: Wipf and Stock Publishers), 14–32.
6 Becca Whitla, *Liberation, (De)Coloniality, and Liturgical Practices: Flipping the Song Bird* (New York: Springer Nature, 2020), 205.
7 Dan Flores, *Coyote America: A Natural and Supernatural History* (New York: Basic Books, 2016).
8 Karen González, "Women Are the First Liberators in the Exodus Story," *Sojourners*, April 16, 2019, https://sojo.net/articles/women-are-first-liberators -exodus-story.
9 Exodus 15:20.
10 Micah 6:4.
11 Renita J. Weems, *Just a Sister Away: Understanding the Timeless Connection Between Women of Today and Women in the Bible* (New York: Grand Central Publishing, 2007).
12 A pseudonym.

CONCLUSION

1 Shelly Rambo, *Resurrecting Wounds: Living in the Afterlife of Trauma* (Waco, TX: Baylor University Press, 2017).
2 Rambo, *Resurrecting Wounds.*
3 This largely came from my introduction to the scholarship of George Eldon Ladd. See George Eldon Ladd, *A Theology of the New Testament* (Grand Rapids, MI: Eerdmans, 1993).
4 Simon Chan, *Liturgical Theology: The Church as Worshiping Community* (Downers Grove, IL: InterVarsity Press, 2009), 37.
5 Filipe Maia, *Trading Futures: A Theological Critique of Financialized Capitalism* (Durham, NC: Duke University Press, 2022).
6 Maia, *Trading Futures*, 1.
7 Eldin Villafane, *The Liberating Spirit: Toward an Hispanic American Pentecostal Social Ethic* (Eugene, OR: Wipf and Stock Publishers, 2021), 198.
8 John 3:8.

Bibliography

Acosta, Larry. "Letting God Change You." Presented at the 68th Annual Missions Conference, Biola University, April 16, 1997. https://digitalcommons.biola.edu/missions-conference/MC1997/mc1997sch/4.

Agius Vallejo, Jody. *Barrios to Burbs: The Making of the Mexican-American Middle Class.* Stanford, CA: Stanford University Press, 2012.

Alexander, Estrelda Y. *Black Fire: One Hundred Years of African American Pentecostalism.* Downers Grove, IL: InterVarsity Press, 2011.

Alonso, Antonio Eduardo. "Latinx Contributions to Liturgical and Sacramental Theology." In *The Wiley Blackwell Companion to Latinoax Theology*, edited by Orlando O. Espín, 292–310. Wiley, 2023. https://doi.org/10.1002/9781119870333.ch16.

Alviso, J. Ricardo. "Feel the Power." *Ethnomusicology Review* 10 (2002): 62–79.

Ammerman, Nancy Tatom. *Studying Lived Religion.* New York University Press, 2021. http://www.degruyter.com/document/isbn/9781479804283/html.

Anzaldúa, Gloria. *Borderlands.* San Francisco: Aunt Lute Books, 1999.

Aponte, Edwin David. *¡Santo!: Varieties of Latino/a Spirituality.* Maryknoll, NY: Orbis Books, 2012.

———."Understanding Spirituality and Theologizing Popular Protestantism." In *The Wiley Blackwell Companion to Latinoax Theology*, edited by Orlando O. Espín, 472–490. Wiley, 2023. https://doi.org/10.1002/9781119870333.ch26.

Armas, Kat. *Abuelita Faith: What Women on the Margins Teach Us about Wisdom, Persistence, and Strength.* Grand Rapids, MI: Brazos Press, 2021.

Badillo, David A. *Latinos and the New Immigrant Church.* Baltimore, MD: Johns Hopkins University Press, 2008.

Barba, Lloyd. "The Borderlands Aesthetics of Mexican American Pentecostalism." In *Protestant Aesthetics and the Arts*, edited by Sarah Covington and Kathryn Reklis, 252–264. New York: Routledge, 2020.

Barba, Lloyd Daniel. *Sowing the Sacred: Mexican Pentecostal Farmworkers in California.* New York: Oxford University Press, 2022.

Bartleman, Frank. *Azusa Street.* Newberry, FL: Bridge Logos Foundation, 1980.

Berger, Peter L. *The Sacred Canopy: Elements of a Sociological Theory of Religion.* Garden City, NY: Doubleday, 1967.

Berho, Deborah L., Gerardo Marti, and Mark T. Mulder. "Global Pentecostalism and Ethnic Identity Maintenance among Latino Immigrants: A Case Study of a Guatemalan Neo-Pentecostal Congregation in the Pacific Northwest." *Pneuma* 39, no. 1–2 (2017): 5–33.

Broyles, Bill, Gayle Harrison Hartmann, Thomas E. Sheridan, Gary Paul Nabhan, and Mary Charlotte Thurtle. *Last Water on the Devil's Highway: A Cultural and Natural History of Tinajas Altas*. Tucson: University of Arizona Press, 2014.

Brusco, Elizabeth E. *The Reformation of Machismo: Evangelical Conversion and Gender in Colombia*. Austin: University of Texas Press, 2011.

Busey, Christopher L., and Carolyn Silva. "Troubling the Essentialist Discourse of Brown in Education: The Anti-Black Sociopolitical and Sociohistorical Etymology of Latinxs as a Brown Monolith." *Educational Researcher* 50, no. 3 (2021): 176–186. https://doi.org/10.3102/0013189X20963582.

Camarillo, Albert. *Chicanos in California: A History of Mexican Americans in California*. San Francisco: Boyd & Fraser, 1984.

Carrasco, Davíd. *Religions of Mesoamerica: Second Edition*. Long Grove, IL: Waveland Press, 2013.

Chan, Simon. *Liturgical Theology: The Church as Worshiping Community*. Downers Grove, IL: InterVarsity Press, 2009.

Chesnut, R. Andrew. *Born Again in Brazil: The Pentecostal Boom and the Pathogens of Poverty*. New Brunswick, NJ: Rutgers University Press, 1997.

———. *Competitive Spirits: Latin America's New Religious Economy*. New York: Oxford University Press, 2003.

Christerson, Brad, Korie L. Edwards, and Michael Oluf Emerson. *Against All Odds: The Struggle for Racial Integration in Religious Organizations*. New York: New York University Press, 2005.

Crane, Ken R. *Latino Churches: Faith, Family, and Ethnicity in the Second Generation*. New Americans. New York: LFB Scholarly Publishing, 2003.

Crawley, Ashon T. *Black Pentecostal Breath: The Aesthetics of Possibility*. New York: Fordham University Press, 2016.

Davis, Mike. "Planet of Slums." *New Left Review* 26 (2004): 5.

Day, Keri. *Azusa Reimagined: A Radical Vision of Religious and Democratic Belonging*. Stanford, CT: Stanford University Press, 2022.

———. *Notes of a Native Daughter: Testifying in Theological Education*. Grand Rapids, MI: Wm. B. Eerdmans Publishing, 2021.

Elisha, Omri. "Proximations of Public Religion: Worship, Spiritual Warfare, and the Ritualization of Christian Dance." *American Anthropologist* 119, no. 1 (2017): 73–85. https://doi.org/10.1111/aman.12819.

Emdin, Christopher. "On Innervisions and Becoming in Urban Education: Pentecostal Hip-Hop Pedagogies in the Key of Life." *Review of Education, Pedagogy, and Cultural Studies* 39, no. 1 (2017): 106–119. https://doi.org/10.1080/10714413.2017.1262170.

Emerson, Michael O., and Christian Smith. *Divided by Faith: Evangelical Religion and the Problem of Race in America.* New York: Oxford University Press, 2000.

Espinosa, Gastón. *Latino Pentecostals in America: Faith and Politics in Action.* Cambridge, MA: Harvard University Press, 2014.

———. *William J. Seymour and the Origins of Global Pentecostalism: A Biography and Documentary History.* Durham, NC: Duke University Press, 2014.

Fallas, Amy. "El Pueblo de Israel: Latino Evangélicos and Christian Zionism." *The Revealer* (blog). September 9, 2021. https://therevealer.org/el-pueblo-de-israel-latino-evangelicos-and-christian-zionism/.

Flores, Dan. *Coyote America: A Natural and Supernatural History.* New York: Basic Books, 2016.

Flores, Edward. *God's Gangs: Barrio Ministry, Masculinity, and Gang Recovery.* New York: New York University Press, 2014.

Flores, Richard R. *Los Pastores: History and Performance in the Mexican Shepherds' Play of South Texas.* Washington, DC: Smithsonian, 1995.

Flores, Tatiana. "'Latinidad Is Cancelled' Confronting an Anti-Black Construct." *Latin American and Latinx Visual Culture* 3, no. 3 (2021): 58–79.

Flores-Yeffal, Nadia Yamel. *Migration-Trust Networks: Social Cohesion in Mexican US-Bound Emigration.* College Station: Texas A&M University Press, 2013. http://muse.jhu.edu/book/23152.

Gault, Erika D., and Travis Harris. *Beyond Christian Hip Hop: A Move Towards Christians and Hip Hop.* New York: Routledge, 2019.

Gill, Jon Ivan. *Underground Rap as Religion: A Theopoetic Examination of a Process Aesthetic Religion.* New York: Routledge, 2019.

González, Karen. "Women Are the First Liberators in the Exodus Story." *Sojourners*, April 16, 2019. https://sojo.net/articles/women-are-first-liberators-exodus-story.

Gustafson, David M. "Pentecostal Evangelist Cenna Osterberg and the Azusa Street Mission." *Pietisten* 35, no. 2 (2020). http://www.pietisten.org/xxxv/2/cenna_osterberg.html.

Guzman, Melissa. "Sanctifying the Expansion of Carceral Control: Spiritual Supervision in the Religious Lives of Criminalized Latinas." *Punishment and Society* 22, no. 5 (June 2020): 681–702. https://doi.org/10.1177/1462474520925328.

Havrelock, Rachel. *River Jordan: The Mythology of a Dividing Line.* Chicago: University of Chicago Press, 2011.

Hervieu-Léger, Danièle, and John A. Farhat. "Religion as Memory: Reference to Tradition and the Constitution of a Heritage of Belief in Modern Societies." In *Religion: Beyond a Concept*, edited by Hent de Vries, 245–258. Fordham University, 2008. http://www.jstor.org/stable/j.ctt1c5chhf.11.

Hicks, Jerry. "Buena Park High Teaches Lesson in the 3 Rs: Resolve, Respect and Reconciliation." *Los Angeles Times*, May 7, 1998, sec. California. https://www.latimes.com/archives/la-xpm-1998-may-07-me-47199-story.html.

Hidalgo, Jacqueline M. "'So Many of Our Destinies Are Tied beyond Our Understanding.' Rethinking Religious Hybridity in Latinx/o/a Contexts." *Missiology* 50, no. 1 (2022): 17–26. https://doi.org/10.1177/009182962110 41047.

Hodge, Daniel White. *Hip Hop's Hostile Gospel: A Post-Soul Theological Exploration.* Boston, MA: Brill, 2016.

Hodges, Melvin L. *The Indigenous Church.* Springfield, MO: Gospel Publishing House, 1976.

Holland, Clifton L. *The Religious Dimension in Hispanic Los Angeles: A Protestant Case Study.* Pasadena, CA: William Carey Library, 1974.

Hondagneu-Sotelo, Pierrette, and Walter Thompson-Hernandez. "Being Brown, Knowing Black." In *South Central Dreams: Finding Home and Building Community in South LA,* edited by Pierrette Hondagneu-Sotelo and Manuel Pastor, 117–154. New York: New York University Press, 2021.

Hooker, Juliet. "Hybrid Subjectivities, Latin American Mestizaje, and Latino Political Thought on Race." *Politics, Groups, and Identities* 2 (June 2014): 188–201. https://doi.org/10.1080/21565503.2014.904798.

Isasi-Díaz, Ada María. *La Lucha Continues: Mujerista Theology.* Maryknoll, NY: Orbis Books, 1996.

Jimenez, Tomas. *Replenished Ethnicity: Mexican Americans, Immigration, and Identity.* Berkeley: University of California Press, 2010.

Khabeer, Su'ad Abdul. *Muslim Cool: Race, Religion, and Hip Hop in the United States.* New York: New York University Press, 2016.

Leon, Luis. "Born Again in East LA: The Congregation as Border Space." In *Gatherings in Diaspora: Religious Communities and the New Immigration,* edited by R. Stephen Warner and Judith G. Wittner, 163–196. Philadelphia: Temple University Press, 1998.

León, Luis D. *La Llorona's Children: Religion, Life, and Death in the U.S.–Mexican Borderlands.* Berkeley: University of California Press, 2004.

Lin, Tony Tian-Ren. *Prosperity Gospel Latinos and Their American Dream.* Chapel Hill: UNC Press Books, 2020.

Little, Emerson. "Recognizing the History behind the Bernal House." *Fullerton Observer,* June 11, 2020. https://fullertonobserver.com/2020/06/11/recognizing-the-history-behind-the-bernal-house/.

Luhrmann, T. M. *When God Talks Back: Understanding the American Evangelical Relationship with God.* New York: Knopf Doubleday Publishing Group, 2012.

Machado, Daisy L. "The Unnamed Woman: Justice, Feminists, and the Undocumented Woman." In *A Reader in Latina Feminist Theology,* edited by María Pilar Aquino, Daisy L. Machado, and Jeanette Rodríguez, 161–176. Austin: University of Texas Press, 2010. https://doi.org/10.7560/705098-010.

Maduro, Otto. "Becoming Pastora: Latina Pentecostal Women's Stories from Newark, New Jersey." *Global Pentecostal Movements* (January 2012): 195–210. https://doi.org/10.1163/9789004235564_011.

Maia, Filipe. *Trading Futures: A Theological Critique of Financialized Capitalism*. Durham, NC: Duke University Press, 2022.

Martell-Otero, Loida, Zaida Maldonado Pérez, and Elizabeth Conde-Frazier. *Latina Evangélicas: A Theological Survey from the Margins*. Eugene, OR: Wipf and Stock Publishers, 2013.

Martí, Gerardo. "Maranatha (O Lord, Come): The Power–Surrender Dynamic of Pentecostal Worship." *Liturgy* 33, no. 3 (2018): 20–28. https://doi.org/10.1080/0458063X.2018.1449515.

———. *Worship across the Racial Divide: Religious Music and the Multiracial Congregation*. New York: Oxford University Press, 2012.

Martinez, Juan F. "Remittances and Mission: Transnational Latino Pentecostal Ministry in Los Angeles." In *Spirit and Power: The Growth and Global Impact of Pentecostalism*, edited by Donald E. Miller, Kimon H. Sargeant, and Richard Flory, 204–223. New York: Oxford University Press, 2013.

Martinez, Juan F., and Lindy Scott. *Los Evangelicos: Portraits of Latino Protestantism in the United States*. Eugene, OR: Wipf and Stock Publishers, 2009.

Matovina, Timothy. *Latino Catholicism: Transformation in America's Largest Church*. Princeton, NJ: Princeton University Press, 2011.

McRoberts, Omar M. *Streets of Glory: Church and Community in a Black Urban Neighborhood*. Chicago: University of Chicago Press, 2003.

Minnis, Paul E., and Michael E. Whalen. *Ancient Paquimé and the Casas Grandes World*. Tucson: University of Arizona Press, 2015.

Mulder, Mark T., Aida I. Ramos, and Gerardo Martí. *Latino Protestants in America: Growing and Diverse*. Lanham, MD: Rowman & Littlefield, 2017.

Nava, Alejandro. *Street Scriptures: Between God and Hip-Hop*. Chicago: University of Chicago Press, 2022. https://doi.org/10.7208/chicago/9780226819150.001.0001.

Ochoa, Gilda L. *Becoming Neighbors in a Mexican American Community: Power, Conflict, and Solidarity*. Austin: University of Texas Press, 2004.

Offutt, Stephen. *Blood Entanglements: Evangelicals and Gangs in El Salvador*. New York: Oxford University Press, 2023.

Orsi, Robert A. *Gods of the City: Religion and the American Urban Landscape*. Bloomington: Indiana University Press.

Payne, Leah. *Gender and Pentecostal Revivalism: Making a Female Ministry in the Early Twentieth Century*. New York: Springer, 2015.

Peña, Elaine. *Performing Piety: Making Space Sacred with the Virgin of Guadalupe*. Berkeley: University of California Press, 2011.

Pérez, Zaida Maldonado. "Dancing with the Wild Child." In *Latina Evangélicas: A Theological Survey from the Margins*, edited by Loida Martell-Otero, Zaida Maldonado Pérez, and Elizabeth Conde-Frazier, 14–32. Eugene, OR: Wipf and Stock Publishers, 2013.

Perry, Imani. *Prophets of the Hood: Politics and Poetics in Hip Hop*. Durham, NC: Duke University Press, 2004.

Pitt, Richard N. *Divine Callings: Understanding the Call to Ministry in Bluck Pentecostalism*. New York: New York University Press, 2012.

Poloma, Margaret, and John Green. *The Assemblies of God : Godly Love and the Revitalization of American Pentecostalism*. New York: New York University Press, 2010.

Premawardhana, Devaka. *Faith in Flux: Pentecostalism and Mobility in Rural Mozambique*. Philadelphia: University of Pennsylvania Press, 2018.

Rambo, Shelly. *Resurrecting Wounds: Living in the Afterlife of Trauma*. Waco, Texas: Baylor University Press, 2017.

Ramírez, Daniel. "Alabaré a Mi Señor: Culture and Ideology in Latino Protestant Hymnody." In *Los Evangelicos: Portraits of Latino Protantism in the United States*, edited by Juan F. Martinez and Lindy Scott, 149–170. Eugene, OR: Wipf and Stock Publishers, 2009.

Ramírez, Daniel. *Migrating Faith: Pentecostalism in the United States and Mexico in the Twentieth Century*. Chapel Hill: UNC Press Books, 2015.

Ramos, Aida I., Gerardo Martí, and Mark T. Mulder. "The Strategic Practice of 'Fiesta' in a Latino Protestant Church: Religious Racialization and the Performance of Ethnic Identity." *Journal for the Scientific Study of Religion* 59, no. 1 (2020): 161–179. https://doi.org/10.1111/jssr.12646.

Reyes, Patrick B. *Nobody Cries When We Die: God, Community, and Surviving to Adulthood*. St. Louis: Chalice Press, 2016.

———. *The Purpose Gap: Empowering Communities of Color to Find Meaning and Thrive*. Westminster, UK: John Knox Press, 2021.

Ríos, Elizabeth D. "'The Ladies Are Warriors': Latina Pentecostalism and Faith-Based Activism in New York City." In *Latino Religions and Civic Activism in the United States*, 197–214. 2005. https://doi.org/10.1093/acpro f:oso/9780195162271.003.0013.

Rivera, Raquel Z. *New York Ricans from the Hip Hop Zone*. New York: Palgrave Macmillan, 2003.

Robbins, Joel. "The Globalization of Pentecostal and Charismatic Christianity." *Annual Review of Anthropology* 33, no. 1 (2004): 117–143. https://doi .org/10.1146/annurev.anthro.32.061002.093421.

Romero, Robert Chao. *Brown Church: Five Centuries of Latina/o Social Justice, Theology, and Identity*. Downers Grove, IL: InterVarsity Press, 2020.

Romero, Robert Chao, and Jeff Liou. *Christianity and Critical Race Theory: A Faithful and Constructive Conversation*. Grand Rapids, MI: Baker Academic, 2023.

Sanchez-Walsh, Arlene. *Latino Pentecostal Identity: Evangelical Faith, Self, and Society*. New York: Columbia University Press, 2003.

Savage, Robert Carlton, ed. *Favoritos Juveniles: Los Himnos y Coritos Más Populares entre la Juventud Latinoamericana*. Grand Rapids, MI: Musica Singspiracion, 1973.

Sorett, Josef. "'It's Not the Beat, but It's the Word That Sets the People Free': Race, Technology, and Theology in the Emergence of Christian Rap Music." *Pneuma* 33, no. 2 (2011): 200–217. https://doi.org/10.1163/027209611X575014.

Sostaita, Barbara. "Borrando La Frontera: Ana Teresa Fernández's Border Communion." In *The Routledge Handbook of Material Religion*, edited by Pooyan Tamimi Arab, Jennifer Scheper Hughes, and S. Brent Rodríguez-Plate, 360–370. New York: Routledge, 2023.

Sostaita, Barbara Andrea. "'Water, Not Walls:' Toward a Religious Study of Life That Defies Borders." *American Religion* 1, no. 2 (2019): 74–97.

Spener, David. *Clandestine Crossings: Migrants and Coyotes on the Texas-Mexico Border*. Ithaca, NY: Cornell University Press, 2011.

Tarango, Angela. *Choosing the Jesus Way: American Indian Pentecostals and the Fight for the Indigenous Principle*. Chapel Hill: UNC Press Books, 2014.

Turner, Victor. *The Ritual Process: Structure and Anti-Structure*. New York: Routledge, 1995. https://doi.org/10.4324/9781315134666.

Tweed, Thomas A. *Crossing and Dwelling: A Theory of Religion*. Cambridge, MA: Harvard University Press, 2009.

VanPool, Todd L, and Christine S. VanPool. "Visiting the Horned Serpent's Home: A Relational Analysis of Paquimé as a Pilgrimage Site in the North American Southwest." *Journal of Social Archaeology* 18, no. 3 (2018): 306–324. https://doi.org/10.1177/1469605318762819.

Vila, Pablo. *Border Identifications: Narratives of Religion, Gender, and Class on the U.S.-Mexico Border*. Austin: University of Texas Press, 2005.

Villafane, Eldin. *The Liberating Spirit: Toward an Hispanic American Pentecostal Social Ethic*. Eugene, OR: Wipf and Stock Publishers, 1993.

Vondey, Wolfgang. *Pentecostal Theology: Living the Full Gospel*. London: Bloomsbury Publishing, 2017.

Wariboko, Nimi, and L. William Oliverio. "The Society for Pentecostal Studies at 50 Years: Ways Forward for Global Pentecostalism." *Pneuma* 42, no. 3–4 (2020): 327–333. https://doi.org/10.1163/15700747-04203021.

Weems, Renita J. *Just a Sister Away: Understanding the Timeless Connection between Women of Today and Women in the Bible*. New York: Grand Central Publishing, 2007.

Whitla, Becca. *Liberation, (De)Coloniality, and Liturgical Practices: Flipping the Song Bird*. Berlin: Springer Nature, 2020.

Yong, Amos. *Discerning the Spirit(s): A Pentecostal-Charismatic Contribution to Christian Theology of Religions*. Eugene, OR: Wipf and Stock Publishers, 2019.

———. *The Spirit Poured Out on All Flesh: Pentecostalism and the Possibility of Global Theology*. Grand Rapids, MI: Baker Academic, 2005.

———. *Who Is the Holy Spirit: A Walk with the Apostles*. Brewster, MA: Paraclete Press, 2011.

Zaragoza-Petty, Alma. *Chingona: Owning Your Inner Badass for Healing and Justice*. Minneapolis: Broadleaf Books, 2022.

Index